Rites of Passage

Nurturing Boys Into Godly Young Men

A How-To Manual

Irving Tolbert

WESTBOW
PRESS®
A DIVISION OF THOMAS NELSON
& ZONDERVAN

WestBow Press books may be ordered through booksellers or by contacting:

WestBow Press
A Division of Thomas Nelson & Zondervan
1663 Liberty Drive
Bloomington, IN 47403
www.westbowpress.com
844-714-3454

Scripture quotations marked NIV are taken from the Holy Bible, New International Version®, NIV®. Copyright © 1973, 1978, 1984 by Biblica, Inc.™ Used by permission of Zondervan. All rights reserved worldwide.

ISBN: 979-8-3850-0927-5 (sc)
ISBN: 979-8-3850-0926-8 (e)

Library of Congress Control Number: 2023919204

Print information available on the last page.

WestBow Press rev. date: 10/11/2023

Dedicated to the Rites of Passage men, women, boys and families

Proceeds donated to the FCBC Rites of Passage Ministry

Contents

Foreword

Irving had a wonderful childhood. Raised in Kansas City, Missouri, Irving was the youngest in a blended family of eight children. His parents each worked two jobs, served in the church, and partied at week's end. Food and fun filled their home despite the frustrations of being born Black in America. Because there were few opportunities in the Midwest, Irving's mom and dad were saddled with menial labor, which they did with pride because they could provide for their family.

Irving loved playing with his friends in the neighborhood after school. A loud voice calling from the apartment windows summoned him home where he was often gently scolded for the soiled clothes and scuffed shoes. Irving finished his usual household chores of washing dishes and cleaning the house aided by his three older brothers, whom he idolized. The Tolbert boys had a reputation!

Alonzo Tolbert, Irving's father, never knew his dad. As a result, Alonzo was always home for dinner, except during the two years he and his wife separated. Irving was 11 years old. Irving's Mom, Vernell, took Irving with her to Los Angeles, where they stayed with Irving's oldest sister, now an adult with three daughters. His behavior deteriorated into near delinquency in this house full of women! Wisdom prevailed, and Vernell sent Irving home to his father, whose stern gaze was all it took to get Irving back in line. Soon afterward, Vernell returned to Kansas City and reunited with her husband.

Through experience, Irving understands the perils of fatherlessness and the emotional pain that results from what feels like rejection of the worst sort. Every boy needs his dad.

On Saturdays, Irving reluctantly trekked with his dad to luxurious homes to cut lawns and care for the rich folks' yards. They often worked till sundown, and the money Irving earned bought him the expensive shoes and stylish hats he wore to school. Dad bought only the basics. Everything else was up to Irving, and work was how to afford anything extra.

In his spare time, Alonzo was a musician. He directed the men's choir, was a bandleader, and played several stringed instruments—guitar, violin, banjo, and upright bass. His lifestyle of industry and worship left an imprint. Irving inherited his dad's love of music, and in addition to serving on the Elder Board for 33 years to date, he sang in the men's choir until it disbanded during COVID.

Like his dad, Irving is remarkably diligent. Twenty-five years of early-morning Saturdays, nine months of the year online or in-person, is a portrait of faithfulness. His passion is to instill in young boys the qualities he learned that make him the man he is today. Because his dad's work and music prevented him from enjoying leisure activities with his son, Irving credits the men of St. Stephen Baptist Church for making the difference in his life.

Deacon Searles was always available. He coached the church's basketball, football, and baseball teams that practiced in neighborhood parks. When it was time to go to a game, Deacon Searles drove his old woody station wagon from block to block collecting the boys around Brooklyn Avenue. They ran and piled onto the tailgate, feet dangling! Irving never missed Alonzo's face in the crowd because Deacon Searles was there.

Deacon Benny directed the St. Stephen Drum and Bugle Corps Marching Band. "We couldn't wait to wear our emerald uniforms, with gold sashes and plume hats. We were stepping, backs arched, playing our instruments and marching in the parades," boasts Irving, who played the French horn. "We learned discipline and loved the camaraderie of standing tall and performing in unison. We learned to follow instructions, execute commands, and stick together. We were a tight group—a family!"

Because of the investment of these deacons, the boys loved going to church. Here is the seed of a ministry that has touched the hearts of hundreds of boys over the past 25 years.

I am amazed at all who serve in the Rites of Passage Ministry (ROP). They are determined to be present in the lives of young men whose memory of their own fathers fades like a mist. In addition to being on the scene every week—often after challenging nine-to-five jobs—these men and women spend hours planning and organizing the year, events, special days, picnics, outings, graduation, and more.

The Village Elders love the Lord, cherish their families, and are pillars of the church and community. Ask any of the wives who keep dinner warm for two hours waiting for the one-hour meeting to end, and you will hear similar applause. And with their finesse, the Parent Council diligently attends to the details that lend such polish to this ministry.

It's impossible to name everyone who makes ROP what it is today, but two names represent the many. Elder Jack Lightsy, Co-Chair/Program Director, serves alongside my husband. His diligence and precision seasoned with respect are priceless. Cherise Davis, Director of the Parent Council, demonstrates her administrative excellence evident on the forms and documents we modified for this book.

Three more names deserve special mention. These outstanding instructors have been teaching for 25 years! Elder Jay Jefferson teaches abstinence education and social skills; Erique Earle Emel, MD, is a pediatrics specialist who teaches health education; and Willie E. Dye, Ph.D., is a biblical archaeologist who teaches creation evidence.

God honors their work and labor of love. The vision of encouraging boys to mature into godly young men is fertile ground. May the Lord restore families with fathers who will never walk away from their sons and mothers who will never push fathers away from their children!

Blessings,
La Verne Tolbert, Ph.D.

Introduction

The Power of One

Tell the older men to be temperate, serious, prudent, and sound in faith, in love, and in endurance....
Likewise, urge the younger men to be self-controlled. (Titus 2:1, 6)

One woman started it all.

Mrs. Sylvia Gaston's son, Kim Gaston, was about to turn 13 years old. She asked the male leaders in our church—the elders and deacons—to impart their godly wisdom to her child. Over several months, we met with her son every week evaluating what it takes for a man to fulfill God's purpose in his life. We instilled principles to help him avoid the traps of gangs, promiscuity, drugs, alcohol, and aimlessness—pitfalls that sideline so many of our youth.

After five months, we called ourselves Village Elders and held a ceremony to mark this young man's transition from boyhood into manhood. This lone graduate echoed the need of thousands of boys.

Following our experience, we met with the Christian Education Pastor and discussed starting a church ministry. It took two years to develop our proposal. Once approved, we recruited boys and volunteers and began the step-by-step process of becoming what we are today.

The Rites of Passage Ministry (ROP) plays a pivotal role in the lives of African-American boys, especially those raised in single-parent homes. We instill into these fertile hearts and minds the truth of God's Word and the reality that God has a purpose for their lives. Armed with the right tools and supported by committed Champions, we equip young men to master life skills as they transition from childhood to manhood.

I compiled this how-to manual in response to the many requests from pastors and leaders who want to start a similar ministry. ROP's ministry leaders developed the documents over the years. We are constantly assessing and updating our policies and procedures to remain in step with the demands of a growing ministry. Reflected here are years of contributions by dedicated members of the ROP team, who are too numerous to name. These leaders are the reason for ROP's success.

The program began in 1998. Over the decades, we've seen young men mature with skills that benefit their lives, families, churches, and communities. They are doctors, entrepreneurs, husbands and fathers, service members, and leaders. We are humbled and honored to have had a part in modeling manhood and speaking into their lives.

The ROP ministry is grateful for the support of Bishop Kenneth C. Ulmer, former pastor of Faithful Central Bible Church in Inglewood, California. During one of his visits to South Africa, he saw a manhood ceremony and returned to share aspects of it with us, which we incorporated into our graduation ceremony. We are grateful to Pastor John Paul Foster, Ph.D., who actively supports and continues the work of the men and women who laid the foundation. Our ministry is biblically based and centers on the redemptive work of our Lord and Savior, Jesus Christ.

The good news of the Gospel is at the core of ROP. Weekly prayer and Bible study engage and equip young men with the Word of God. In addition, a dedicated ROP women's prayer team faithfully intercedes for the leadership and participants. Because of their commitment, we have seen God's handiwork through the years. How blessed we are that the Father entrusts us with the opportunity to lead as role models as we follow in His steps. May your ministry flourish as you change lives, one boy at a time!

Elder Irving H. Tolbert, D.Div., Chairman

Standing rear, right to left: Sheila Lightsy (family friend, her husband Don, is the photographer); Derek and Amy Jones (family friends); Elder Irving and Dr. La Verne Tolbert; Odette Kahwajian (family friend); Grandson Josiah Garrison; La Nej and Matt Garrison (daughter and son-in-law). Seated right to left: Grandsons Judah and Jeremiah Garrison; Len and Olga Chandler (family friends); Granddaughter Faith Tolbert (daughter of Catrice Tolbert). *Photo: Don Lightsy during the November 3, 2018, ROP Graduation at Faithful Central Bible Church, Inglewood, Los Angeles.*

Chapter 1

A Lesson from Elephants—Why ROP

In Pilanesberg, South Africa, the solution to reducing the elephant population was to slaughter the older elephants. Young elephants or calves were left to survive on their own. The young adolescents, full of aggression, banded together. These six-ton teenagers went on a rampage, destroying property and killing over 50 rhinos, brutally mutilating their carcasses. They were running wild, and the situation was entirely out of control.

The solution was to import six adult male elephants or bulls from Kruger National Park. It didn't take long for the old bulls to establish order. Within hours, the adolescents, who previously had no example of proper adult behavior, settled down and became socialized.

The lesson is clear: Older, mature elephants are essential to model how to behave.

Missing Warriors

Warriors are missing from the village. According to the National Center for Fathering, more than 20 million children go to bed without a father present. Says Dr. Ken Canfield, a pioneer in fatherhood research, "Fatherlessness continues to be one of the most pressing social issues of our time. With the growing complexities in families and fathering situations, the need for effort and attention in this area is even greater."[1]

According to the National Center for Fathering:[2]

- **An estimated 24.7 million children (33%) live absent from their biological father.** *U.S. Census Bureau, Current Population Survey*, "Living Arrangements of Children under 18 Years/1 and Marital Status of Parents by Age, Sex, Race, and Hispanic Origin and Selected Characteristics of the Child for all Children 2010." Table C3. Internet Release Date November 2010. https://www.census.gov/data/tables/2010/demo/families/cps-2010.html

- **Of students in grades 1 through 12, 39% (17.7 million) live in homes absent from their biological fathers.** Nord, Christine Winquist, and West, Jerry. *Fathers' and Mothers' Involvement in their Children's Schools by Family Type and Resident Status.* Table 1. (NCES 2001-032). Washington, DC: U.S. Department of Education, National Center of Education Statistics, 2001. https://nces.ed.gov/pubs2001/2001032.pdf

- **57.6% of black children, 31.2% of Hispanic children, and 20.7% of white children live absent from their biological fathers.** *Family Structure and Children's Living Arrangements 2012.* Current Population Report. U.S. Census Bureau, July 1, 2012. https://fathers.com/the-extent-of-fatherlessness/

- **According to a poll of the U.S. population, 72.2% believe that fatherlessness is America's most significant family or social problem.** The National Center for Fathering (NCF), "Fathering in America Poll," January 1999. https://fathers.com/statistics-and-research/the-extent-of-fatherlessness/

Divorce and out-of-wedlock births are significant causes of fatherlessness. The remnants of slavery, the brutality of racism, and the ignorance of discrimination systematically designed to disenfranchise an entire people are underlying factors resulting in educational and economic disparities, joblessness and welfare, disproportionate rates in the foster care system, and the disproportionality of Black male incarceration.

> Sadly, today as you look around the village you will find that there is an element of major importance absent. It is nationally estimated that tonight 40% (25 million) of the children will go to bed without a father present in the home. In Black America that statistic rises to over 50% and in some urban settings it rises as high as 90%. The repercussion of this absence should concern us. The children remain the victims.

> To understand the impact of this absence on the children requires an understanding of the role of the father in the village. By our Creator's design, fathers have long

---

[1] Canfield, Ken. "The Village Warriors Return." https://fathers.com/about-ncf/our-history/

[2] https://fathers.com/the-extent-of-fatherlessness/

been given the responsibility as primary protectors, providers, blessers and leaders of the family. They are the warriors, the ones engaged and experienced in battles against anything that seeks to harm or divide their families.

What happens when the warriors are missing? The enemies of the village come in to steal, to kill and to destroy. When we look around our black villages we see the aftermath of destruction upon our children and families. We see record levels of poverty, violence, low educational achievement, teenage pregnancy, crime, substance abuse and suicide. According to current research most of these outcomes are strongly related to father absent homes.[3]

Jesus has come "that we might have life, and that more abundantly" (John 10:10). With godly role models, the destruction of children and families can be stemmed and reversed. ROP is determined to do its small part to eliminate poverty, avert violence, reverse low educational achievement, erase abortion, and reduce crime, substance abuse, and suicide—shreds of evidence in father-absent homes.

Village Warriors Return

It is time for the village warriors to return. ROP men and women leaders are determined to stay. Our communities deserve the investment of time. God will turn the father's hearts toward their children (Malachi 3:6).

The men volunteering in ROP are neither replacing nor filling the gap for absent or negligent fathers. Like adult male elephants, ROP serves as godly role models. Village Elders, Champions, and Instructors help boys navigate to adulthood. ROP walks alongside fathers present in their boys' lives and fathers who live in the home to support and involve them in the program. Each year, ROP selects an outstanding dad to receive an award as "Father of the Year."

The program helps develop boys into mature, productive men who love the Lord, love their wives, become fathers, protect their families, and lead their households in the fear and admonition of the Lord. With boys, fathers, mothers, and a team of volunteers, ROP has ministered for over 25 years and counting!

This chapter is the *why* of ROP. The following chapters outline the way ROP works. We give all glory to God for the vision he has placed on our hearts...and yours.

> Now to Him who is able to keep you from stumbling, and to present you faultless before the presence of His glory with exceeding joy, to God our Savior, who alone is wise, be glory and majesty, dominion and power, both now and forever. Amen. (Jude 1:24–25, NKJV)

---

[3]   Williams, George R. "The Village Warriors Return." https://fathers.com/s5-yoursituation/urban-fathering/the-village-warriors-return-2/)

Chapter 2

The Way It Works—Ministry Overview

The model for ROP is the African tribal tradition. In the Motherland, young boys leave their mothers and go with the older men into the bush. Armed with lessons from family life and adults in the village, these soon-to-be young men abandon the familiar to face challenges that build confidence, fortitude, and respect as they learn cooperation and independence. After a challenging season away from the nurturing eye of mother, the boys return home to the applause of the entire village. There's a celebration because these young men are ready to protect and help provide for their families and community.

Approximately 25% of the Initiates are from intact families, and their fathers participate as mentors or champions. However, most of the Initiates are from single-parent female-headed households. Society considers these boys "at risk," but ROP is determined to snatch these boys from the clutches of the negative psychological and emotional consequences that result from fatherlessness. Single mothers especially benefit when the village partners with them to help nurture their sons.

> I sincerely believe that it takes a man to develop boys into men…I did not say a single female parent could not develop her son into a man, but she does not need to attempt such a significant act alone.…Very few African American women are consciously aware that their son needs a positive role model, that the family, streets, television, school and church institutions come up lacking, and that a concerted effort between them and a male extended family member must actively fill the void. Until African American women admit that only men can make boys into men, and African American men become responsible for giving direction to at least one male child, the conspiracy [to destroy Black boys] will continue.[4]

According to Kunjufu, a Rites of Passage program is essential for every African American boy. "What prevents us from moving from theory to practice?" On the author's list as number one is "lack of information."[5] Our goal is to provide the basic information you need to start your ministry today.

---

[4] Kunjufu, Jawanza. *Countering the Conspiracy to Destroy Black Boys*. Revised Edition: African American Images. p. 59
[5] ibid.

Goal and Objectives

ROP is a discipleship program that promotes a healthy transition from boyhood to manhood.[6] Our goal is to provide biblical principles that equip young men with practical strategies to handle life's temptations as they develop into godly young men.

To accomplish the goal, ROP has identified five objectives: spiritual, educational, social, physical, and vocational.

1. Spiritual—Deepen their relationship with the Lord by reading, studying, and being guided by God's Word.
2. Educational—Determine to excel in school by sharpening study habits that ensure success.
3. Social—Decide to cultivate positive relationships by respecting parents, siblings, peers, and treating girls and women with godly respect.
4. Physical—Dedicate time to exercise by committing to a disciplined schedule.
5. Vocational—Develop life skills by exploring topics relevant to society today.

A well-rounded curriculum addresses these areas: prayer and Bible (spiritual); study habits, test preparation and goal setting (educational); etiquette and attire, including how to be a gentleman, first aid and CPR (social); military drill, health and hygiene, sexual abstinence and STD/STIs (physical); biblical anthropology, introduction to space, careers in engineering, principles of success, finance and management principles, trades and crafts mechanics, home maintenance, plumbing, auto repair, graphic illustration and the arts (vocational).

March to October

The ROP program requires an 8-month commitment (March through October) for boys 12 to 15 years old, whom we call Initiates. Families from churches around the city, country, and globe (thanks to the Internet) are welcome to participate.

Global ROP

ROP is now global. We average 32 boys each year, but during the COVID pandemic, we held online meetings and had our largest class ever—52 Initiates! Global ROP was born. The limits of technology are challenging, and although it's a great substitute, nothing is as effective as being there in person.

---

[6] Getz, Gene A. (2016). *The Measure of a Man: Twenty Attributes of a Godly Man*. Revised Edition. Michigan: Revell.

Tiered Leadership

The program has a tiered leadership structure of individuals. We assign each Initiate to a team that includes a Village Elder (VE), Man of Valor (MOV), and a Champion. Each Champion serves as a mentor to one or two Initiates. The Parent Council and Prayer Ministry is comprised of women.

Leaders:

> Pastor (Village Chief)
> > Pastoral Overseer
> > > Chairman of Village Elders
> > > > Vice Chairman of Village Elders
> > > > > Program Director
> > > > > > Treasurer
> > > > > > > Ministry Chaplain
> > > > > > > > Production Director
> > > > > > > > > Physical Training Director
> > > > > > > > > > Marketing Director
> > > > > > > > > > > Education Coordinator

Teams:

Village Elders	**Parent Council**
Men of Valor	Prayer Ministry
Champions	
Instructors	

Role of Leaders

The Senior Pastor is the **Village Chief** who sets the spiritual tone for ROP. He is also the voice of outreach to the boys, parents and community.

The **Pastoral Overseer** assists the senior pastor in accomplishing ROP's goals and is an advisor to the Chairman and Elders. While the Village Chief and Pastoral Overseer are staff, the rest of us are volunteers. We offer our time and resources to the work of the kingdom by serving the Lord through ROP.

As **Chairman**, my role is to oversee ROP and interface with the Village Chief, Pastoral Overseer, and Program Director. I work closely with the Program Director and oversee the Village Elders, the education and training programs, field trips, fund-raising, Graduation Day Ceremony, and the Parent Council. Here are the other roles:

- **Vice Chairman** supports the Chairman and may be his substitute in the Chairman's absence. The Vice Chairman also supervises the classroom instruction and monitors teacher performance and student assignments.

- **Program Director** provides direction for the day-to-day operation of ROP. He interfaces with all levels of leadership, especially the Chairman, Parent Council, MOV, and Champions, organizes and chairs the monthly meetings, coordinates the annual ROP picnic, and oversees the fund-raising activities.
- **Ministry Chaplin** is responsible for the monthly Saturday morning prayer. He also provides support and spiritual counseling to ROP boys and their families, especially during a family crisis.
- **Production Director** organizes and coordinates the programs, such as Mother's/Father's Day and Graduation. He schedules rehearsals and oversees setting up the room or sanctuary.
- **Treasurer** oversees the budget. He is also responsible for ensuring that financial goals are met through fundraising.
- **Physical Training Director** leads the morning drill and physical training and supervises discipline and detention. With his recommendation, Initiates are promoted in rank.
- **Marketing Director** promotes the program to the community and assists with fund-raising by securing non-obligatory sponsors.
- **Education Coordinator** is responsible for the classroom instruction, including curriculum, interviews, and selection of instructors and course material. He also monitors the instructors and coordinates the bi-monthly tutoring sessions.

Role of Teams

The TEAM model—**T**ogether **E**veryone **A**chieves **M**ore—is how we function. We band together, work together, and support one another. **Village Elders** (VE) are the decision-makers who provide leadership to the teams.

- **Men of Valor** (MOV) are Super Champions who have volunteered for ROP several years devoting time and effort as indicators of their commitment. MOVs who demonstrate outstanding leadership become Village Elders.
- **Champions** are mentors who volunteer one year. Each Champion is assigned one or two Initiates. The Champion calls the Initiate weekly to offer encouragement or help with any challenges. Champions become Men of Valor (MOV) when they demonstrate commitment to the vision of ROP by continuing to volunteer beyond their one-year commitment.
- **Instructors** teach the classes during the Saturday ROP training and include professors, archeologists, teachers, entrepreneurs, ministers, and more!

Role of Women

Once we began ROP, it didn't take long for us to realize we can do more with the help of women, especially the mothers who are inspired by their son's success and want to pay it forward.

- **Parent Council** (PC), led by the Director, devotes their efforts to counseling and walking alongside the younger mothers according to the biblical model of the older women helping the younger (Titus 2:4). The PC also provides administrative support and is on duty every week signing in the boys, encouraging parental participation, coordinating the application and intake, and preparing meals and snacks.
- **Prayer Team** is a ministry of the Parent Council. The Chaplain leads these praying women to intercede for the volunteers, boys, and their families. And do they pray!

It's easy to understand that with their charm and finesse, women contribute to the exceptional quality of our program. Their participation and encouragement are priceless. Together, the women and men sacrifice their time, talent and treasure to make ROP what it is today.

If this organizational structure and explanation seem overwhelming, remember we started ROP with a few elders, one mom, and one boy. Over the years we added positions, teams, and more. It's amazing how God equips the Church with people who have such a variety of skills, gifts, and talents. Listening to their ideas and suggestions is the best way to grow your ministry.

Are you ready to explore a calendar year? Excellent! We'll review the eight-month program in the next chapter.

MINISTRY MEN

Leap of Faith – Team 1

God's Plan — Team 2

Trinity – Team 3

Mustard Seed — Team 4

Village Elders: Dwayne Fuqua, Irving Tolbert, Jack Lightsy, James Alexander, Jimmy (JW) White, Ron Williams, Stephan Tucker, Tomas Johnson, Urel McGill

Men of Valor: Donn Hobbs, Harrison Wambulu, Lloyd Walker, Robert Auten, Terry Duplessis

Champions: Alan Gaines, Alex Sands, Calvin Mauldin, Carlos Ray, Craig Bracey-Dokes, Demetrius Howze, Don Owens, Dylan Hunter, Ed Tillman, Jalen Gray, James Bolden, Jay Jefferson, Jay Tryon, Jeffrey Brown, Keith Anglin, Keith Harrison, Kenneth Giles, Kenneth Martin, III, Nigel Francis, Robert Patterson, Robert Webb, Tie Richards, Tyron Auston

morning drill

PARENT COUNCIL

Aisha Mitchell	Cherise Williams	Kimberly Phillips	Renee Atkinson
Angie Anglin	Christian Reed	LaShon Rayford	Shameka McCoy
Arletha Ross	Clarisa Walker	LaVonda Storrs	Sheryl Lightsy
Beverly Pannell	Desserie Jones	Lenda McGill	Terry Gilbert
Candice Maroney	Gessille Jensen	Marilyn Lightsy	Vernette Williams
Cassandra Reed	Janice Henderson	Melandie Austin	Yvette Evans
Cherise Davis	Keana Clay	Myra Lightsy	Yvonne Parker

PRAYER TEAM
& Guest Speakers

In everything you do, put God first, and he will direct you and crown your efforts with success.
Proverbs 3:6 (TLB)

As followers of Christ, we should all aspire to spend more time in the presence of God so that we might discover more about the heart and will of God. And the knowledge we gain should not just be for the sake of learning. It should be applied to our lives.

Chapter 3

Eight Months—The Program Schedule

We dedicate 33 Saturdays to the program, not including holiday weekends. We begin the first day with an inspection followed by two hours of physical training and two hours of classroom instruction. We also plan outings, field trips, and tours during the eight-month program. We conclude the program with a graduation ceremony to celebrate our hard work.

Weekly Bible Study

Weekly Bible study is essential to building these young men in the most critical area—their spiritual development. The Word of God guides and encourages excellence. Without the Lord's help and direction, everything else is meaningless. We mentor by depositing biblical principles that are good enough to last a lifetime.

It's true that "iron sharpens iron" (Proverbs 27:17). The most devoted teacher can sharpen his or her skills by learning how students learn and employing effective teaching methodology for engaging, memorable lessons. The women and men in our program completed teacher training to teach so that learners learn.[7] We limit lectures by asking questions, telling stories, playing videos, using arts and crafts, demonstrating with show and tell, capitalizing on teachable moments, and more!

During the week, mentors call their Initiate to see how the week progresses. It's the best opportunity to remind the boys about the previous Bible lesson and ask if they have any questions. When homework assignments involve Bible study, we're there to help.[8] Discussing God's Word models what we value most.

The *Africa Study Bible* combines biblical study with Black History! There isn't a more effective way of teaching God's Word in its proper context since many biblical events occurred in and around the African continent. God has given us a valuable tool with research and stories about our culture and context.[9]

---

[7]   Tolbert, La Verne. (2000). *Teaching Like Jesus: A Practical Guide to Christian Education In Your Church*. Grand Rapids: Zondervan.

[8]   Tolbert, La Verne. (2019). *How to STUDY and Understand the Bible in 5 Simple Steps Without Learning Hebrew or Greek*. 2nd Edition. Illinois: Evangelical Training Association. www.etaworld.org

[9]   Jusu, John. Supervising Editor. (2016). *The Africa Study Bible*. Oasis International Limited.

Black History

Studying Black History is another core value to our program. Leaders and guest speakers exemplify current Black history. To spotlight both well-known and unknown history-makers of the past, we take pages from a dynamic little book: *African American Inventions and Inventors* by Baron J. Littleton, Jr.[10]

Here's an example of an activity based on Littleton's book. Divide the boys into teams and have awards for those who score the highest. This Teacher Sheet has the answers in parentheses after each question. [Teacher Sheet: Things that Make You Go Hmmmm!]

[10]   Littleton, Jr., Baron J. (2006). *African American Inventions and Inventors.* Your Little Black Book, Vol 1. Los Angeles: Disciple One Publishing.

Things that make you go "Hmmmm!"

A Review of African American Inventors:

Dr. Shirley Jackson (A)

Frederick McKinley Jones (B)

Marie Van Brittan Brown (C)

Lewis Latimer (D)

Ask students to fill in their answer by writing A, B, C, or D in the blank space.

1. Who invented the roof-mounted cooling system that's used to refrigerate goods on trucks while they are being transported from one place to another? And, his invention keeps vegetables fresh! During World War II, his cooling-system invention also helped to preserve blood. ____B_____ (Frederick McKinley Jones)

2. She was the first African American woman to earn a Ph.D. in physics at MIT. Her inventions helped give us the touch-tone telephone, the portable fax, caller ID, call-waiting, and the fiber optic cable. _____A_____ (Dr. Shirley Jackson)

3. On September 4, 1848, he lit up the world! Working with Thomas Edison his greatest invention was the carbon filament, the part that makes the light bulb light. He also helped Edison with the design of the telephone. And, when it's too hot to stay outside, remember that he designed the air-conditioner. _____D_____ (Lewis Latimer)

4. A nurse, she developed the home security system to alert a resident that someone was at the door. This system had a camera, a monitor, and a peep-hole, along with an alarm button to contact the police, if necessary. Today, because of her invention, we have the modern home-security and closed-circuit TV system, the push-button alarm system, crime prevention, and traffic monitoring. _____C_____ (Marie Van Brittan Brown)

Ask students to circle their score: 25% 50% 75% 100%

Physical Training

The physical training we've selected is military style. Other programs might have sports or athletic activity, but we're in the Army, Navy, or Marines. The men in charge are former Drill Sergeants who served in the armed forces. Their love of discipline, neatness, cleanliness, and hygiene make them excellent role models for the Initiates. The Drill Sergeants' tough love encourages these young men to mature emotionally and mentally.

Initiates begin Basic Training wearing gray sweats and then graduate to wearing military fatigues, boots, and hats. We note those who follow the direction of the drill sergeants and promote them in rank as an example to the other Initiates.

Saturday Schedule

- 6:45 a.m. Sign-in
- 7:00 a.m. Physical Training (Military style)
- 8:45 a.m. Break
- 9:00 a.m. Classroom Instruction (1st class)
- 10:00 a.m. Classroom Instruction (2nd class)
- 11:00 a.m. Sign-out with parent
- 11:30 a.m. Detention if there has been a discipline problem
- 11:30 a.m. Tutoring twice a month to help with school subjects if requested

Every month, ROP provides opportunities for recreational and educational field trips or activities that reinforce by experience and involvement what has been learned and presented in the classroom. Activities are centered in Los Angeles, California and the surrounding area and include activities such as:

- A 6-hour day of service at the LA Union Rescue Mission
- College day campus tour at one of our local universities
- Mother's Day Ceremony
- Tour of NASA JPL
- One week trip to a camp, typically in the San Bernardino Mountains
- Trip to Camp Pendleton Marine Base
- 3-day Grand Canyon/Colorado River trip or 1-day Catalina Island trip
- Compton Courthouse tour
- Space Science Museum (Home of the Space Shuttle Endeavor)
- African-American Museum/African-American Firefighters' Museum
- Annual ROP Picnic
- Graduation Ceremony
- Thanksgiving Boxes of Love

- Christmas Party
- Angel Tree

This is just a partial list to provide an idea of the robust program. A full list of activities/ excursions is in Chapter 5. An example of the Calendar of Events is in Part 2.

As you can see, it takes people—volunteers—to make this all happen. Volunteers are essential to our program's success. How do we recruit? We pray! And this is what we'll discuss in the next chapter.

Chapter 4

Pray for Laborers—Recruitment

The harvest is plentiful, but the laborers—the volunteers—are few. We pray for laborers! We ask Father God to send us men and women volunteers according to Matthew 9:38, "Ask the Lord of the harvest, therefore, to send out workers into his harvest field" (NIV). We pray!

Pray for Encouragers

The Bible is full of excellent examples of encouragers, those who made a difference in another person's life. Remember Saul, also called Paul? Witnesses laid their coats at Saul's feet when the religious rulers threw stones to kill Deacon Stephen (Acts 7). "And Saul approved of their killing him," (Acts 8:1, NIV). On a murderous rampage to persecute Jews who had become followers of Jesus Christ, Saul hunted men and women house by house and dragged them to prison (Acts 8:3).

Here was a young man traveling the wrong way until he was on the road to Damascus. After his blinding encounter with Jesus, Saul became a Christ defender. Unfortunately, his reputation preceded him. The disciples didn't trust Saul, but Barnabas encouraged him.

> Then Barnabas went to Tarsus to look for Saul, and when he found him, he brought him to Antioch. So, for a whole year, Barnabas and Saul met with the church and taught great numbers of people. The disciples were called Christians first at Antioch. (Acts 11:25–26, NIV)

His name was John, but everyone called him by the nickname Barnabas, which means "son of encouragement." And encourage others he did! After splitting with Paul over Mark's immature behavior, Barnabas encouraged Mark and sailed with him to Cyprus (Acts 15:36–41). Mark the Evangelist is the author of the Gospel of Mark. We pray that the Lord will send other sons of encouragement to mentor the next generation.

Wanted: Men of Integrity!

Integrity summarizes what's needed most in a Champion because he is a role model. Lifestyle, reputation, spiritual maturity, and family life combined make the best candidates for Champions. These men may be in your church praying about how their wisdom, experience, and resources can help fulfill the church's vision. They are waiting for an invitation, which is the heart of recruitment.

Men's ministries, such as men's choirs or Bible study, are the best place to begin. And do share the vision with men who meet together in small groups. Of course, announcements on social media or from the pulpit are very effective. Skits and videos are entertaining and compelling if a creative writer is on your team. Repeat the vision and need for volunteers in as many ways as possible. The good news is that volunteers recruit other volunteers, which is the best part of working together in the Kingdom of God.

Once recruitment begins, a VE follows up during the week with a phone call to schedule an interview. Champions will attend a training session and must complete a background check. During the program year, Champions commit to supporting and encouraging their assigned Initiate by calling him once a week.

Listen for volunteers who are committed to the Lord and want to serve Him. Spiritual maturity counts, measured by a quality of life—what volunteers have learned, how they have developed, and their desire to help others. Are they members who regularly attend church? What is significant to their spiritual development? Are they faithful husbands and fathers? Are they employed and contributing to their church and community?

Volunteers' reputations with their families at home and brothers and sisters at church indicate how well they can coach or mentor others. Their example speaks louder than words. With good communication and interpersonal skills and a willing attitude to serve, these Champions will develop relationships with the boys and be valuable contributors to the ROP team.

Champion Duties and Responsibilities

First and foremost, Champions are mentors to the Initiates. Calling the Initiate weekly is one of their most essential duties. Why? The average six-year-old will spend more time watching television and movies than talking to his dad. Hollywood's influence is additional cause for concern.[11] ROP is determined to interrupt this trend by recruiting godly men to speak into the lives of the Initiates.

During the program year, the Champion's wisdom, experience, confidence, insight, social skills, and values help to mature and empower the Initiate. To protect each boy, the Champion, and the church's reputation, Champions should never be alone or have a one-on-one outing with an Initiate. Church policy stipulates the two-adult rule, to which ROP strictly adheres.

---

[11] Wright, Carl Jeffrey. (2004). *God's Vision or Television? How Television Influences What We Believe.* Illinois: UMI.

Consistency is vital. Champions are responsible for supporting their team with bi-weekly attendance on Saturdays. Duties vary from helping in the classroom to serving as a chaperone on outings. We invite all volunteers to attend the monthly ROP prayer and intercession meetings.

Once recruitment and the interview process conclude, the two-hour group training is next. Village Elders and MOVs are present to establish relationships and answer questions. Volunteers also receive information about their uniforms, ROP policy, and how to provide help and encouragement to their Initiate. Like Barnabas with Paul and Mark, one godly Champion will multiply into thousands who will impact the lives of others.

How is a Champion a "son of encouragement"? The Champion is a valuable resource providing information seasoned with wisdom based on years of experience. Each man, equipped with specific skills, talents, and abilities, is chosen by God to listen to the Initiate and provide the feedback he needs. Champions are coaches, and coaches are a sounding board where someone who cares can address ideas, visions, discouragements, and fears. When the Initiate has a challenge at home or school, the Champion helps devise reasonable steps for resolution by asking questions and considering all available options.

The Benefits

It's emotionally fulfilling to honor God by sacrificing the time to serve as a role model for a child. What better opportunity to sharpen and enhance our skills than helping others? Being a role model is a source of personal revitalization and spiritual renewal that benefits both giver and receiver.

Mentoring helps younger men mature and older men rejuvenate. We grow in the process of assisting others to develop. The remarkable result provides the fulfillment that enhances our self-image and God-esteem. If we don't generate new relationships and cultivate new ideas, we'll become stagnant.

In ROP, we are all Champions! How grateful we are that God is using us, and how dependent we are on the wisdom of God to accomplish His will!

Being a Champion is a powerful tool that impacts our church and community, one boy at a time. Our young people need our help! God has chosen us because He trusts us with the challenges we encounter in our elephant-male role.

Now that you've caught the vision, let's discuss how to finance your ROP. Suggestions are in the next chapter.

Chapter 5

Field Trips and Fundraising—Financing the Vision

We underwrite the 33-week program with parent fees, fundraisers, and donations. Parents pay for their sons' uniforms, camp week, and field trips. Those who demonstrate their inability to pay have some costs underwritten by volunteers whose contributions assist needy families. All volunteers pay for their uniforms and field trips.

Field trips are an essential part of ROP. We decide on several outings and sprinkle these trips throughout the program year to bond with the boys. In Southern California, there are lots of options for outdoor activities, including the following:

- African American Firefighter Museum
- Annual Picnic
- Beach
- Bowling
- California African American Museum
- California Science Center
- Compton Courthouse
- Go Kart World
- Grand Canyon National Park
- Intuit Dome
- J. Paul Getty Museum
- Jet Propulsion Laboratory
- Local College Campuses (Biola University, CSU Long Beach, UCLA, USC)
- Los Angeles Dodgers
- Marine Corps Base Camp Pendleton
- Mile High Pines/Alpine Retreat and Camp
- Naval Base San Diego
- Santa Catalina Island
- Sequoia National Park
- Skid Row
- SoFi Stadium
- Union Rescue Mission

We recommend selecting a variety of outings to target everyone's interest. You can also choose excursions that correspond with the theme of your ROP. If it's sports, focus on athletic events. Or, if music, find the best outdoor and indoor venues or concerts. Remember that new experiences may spark new visions, so be creative. You get the idea!

Fundraising

Creative fundraising—from popcorn to pages in the graduation Souvenir book—is vital! Once your church and community understand the vision of ROP—to nurture boys into godly young men—they will be eager to lend their support. Solicit donations from businesses and organizations. For the graduation ceremony, offer opportunities to support ROP by purchasing advertisements in the program. At the annual picnic, raffles are popular, especially when the gifts are excellent.

If your team has a development expert or someone with the gift of grant writing to solicit donations from banks and corporations, you are blessed. It's surprising how many funds are available for those willing to put pen to paper and apply. Invite parents and volunteers to ask their companies or businesses to support the ROP vision with a donation.

Remember, the best way to receive large donations is to send a fund-raising packet in the name of your church's Community Development Corporation (CDC). Every member of your team should send one packet to an athletic team, business, bank, or Christian enterprise. Follow up with a phone call and be diligent about speaking to a live person. Emails are effective, too, but voice-to-voice communication is best.

Don't hesitate to pray, and don't hesitate to ask! Remember, we do not have because we do not ask God (James 4:2). We invite volunteers to present the Fundraising Package to their companies and businesses. It's encouraging to see how well corporations, banks, shops and individuals respond. Every donation, whether large or small, helps make a difference. (See Part 2 for the Fundraising Package.]

Now that we've covered the basics, let's discuss how to start your program year. Begin with a group orientation to remind parents and volunteers of their roles and responsibilities. We'll preview what occurs during orientation in the next chapter.

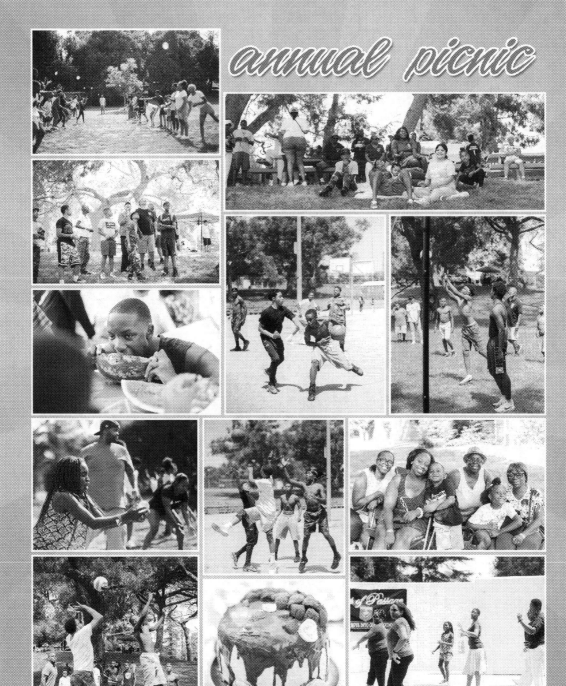

annual picnic

beach
party

INSTRUCTION

Chapter 6

Learning the Ropes—Orientation

Everyone is excited to begin this journey! The festive two-hour Orientation is a time to meet and share the vision with parents, grandparents, and caregivers. Serving breakfast is a warm welcome.

As with every event, demonstrate that you value everyone's investment to attend by beginning and ending on time. Since the program officially starts the next Saturday, parents pay for the program year during Orientation. It's helpful to have badges or nametags to encourage learning everyone's name.

The Senior Pastor or Pastoral Overseer speaks for a few minutes (just a few!) to thank the ROP volunteers and welcome the parents. What a wonderful time to invite anyone "new" to attend Sunday morning service! In this way, the pastor highlights the church's commitment to children, youth, and families.

Next, the Chairman explains the history of ROP and gives an overview of its goals and objectives. Then Village Elders, the Men of Valor, and Champions introduce themselves, along with the Parent Council—the women who will help guide the mothers throughout the ROP year.

Elders take turn discussing aspects of the next eight months. We present an overview of the graduation ceremony to inspire commitment throughout the program. Having the end in sight often helps during those early-morning Saturdays when enthusiasm dwindles. Orientation concludes with a Questions and Answer session before we end in prayer. Here is an example of an Orientation agenda.

Orientation Agenda

1. Sign-in, Fellowship, and Continental Breakfast
2. Opening Prayer and Pastoral Welcome
3. ROP History and Overview – Village Elder, Irving Tolbert
4. Introduction of Village Elders, Men of Valor, and Champions
5. Role of a Champion – Village Elders Stephan Tucker and Bruce Taylor; Men of Valor Robert Auten
6. Biblical Perspective/Bible Study/ROP Prayer Team – Village Elder Omar Muhammad and Chaplain Vernette Williams
7. Overview of Graduation Ceremony – Village Elder Jack Lightsy

8. Physical Training – Sergeants James Alexander/Urel McGill
9. ROP Instruction – Village Elder Ron Williams
   - Bible Study
   - Sexual Abstinence & Life Skills
   - First Aid
   - Health & Hygiene
   - Other Classes
   - Tutoring
   - Outings
10. Alumni Testimony
11. Administrative Items/Parent Council – Village Elder Jack Lightsy and Parent Council, Cherise Davis
12. Champions Breakout
13. Fundraising Events – Village Elder Stephan Tucker
14. Questions & Answers Session
15. Closing Prayer
16. Intake interviews with initiates

Invitation and Attitude

Some families who are interested in ROP also need a church home. Orientation is an ideal time to present the variety of ways that the church supports families. Why not invite leaders from the church's children's and youth ministry, choir, Bible study, small groups, missions, and more to have a table and explain how to join the activities? A welcoming attitude is a wonderful way to witness!

Having an optimistic, upbeat attitude is vital to a successful orientation. We also avoid making promises. The ROP program will instill principles, not perform miracles.

Intake Interviews

Did we mention that the Elders meet with every family enrolling in ROP? Working in teams, we personally interview the mothers and fathers, grandparents, aunts and uncles, caregivers, and the Initiates. We discuss the family composition, the Initiate's relationship with his father and with those in his home, and his successes and challenges at school. Families who missed their interviews may interview after orientation, but we try to keep this number to a minimum.

The interview process ensures that our skills match the families' expectations. We cannot accept every boy, unfortunately. We are volunteers. Although there may be an exception, we are not professionals in social work or the medical field. VEs have intervened to rescue a couple of boys from gang involvement, but our program is not designed for extreme remedial issues such as gang involvement or verbally or physically violent youth. We cannot jeopardize the entire group of boys for the one child who is determined to be destructive or disobedient. Although now might not be the right time, he is always welcome to return next year.

The questions we ask during the Intake Interview are in Part 2. They are a guide to help us determine the parents' commitment level and the boy's motivation to participate. Even boys who enter the program at the persistent nudging of their parents express their gratitude for the opportunity and experience of ROP once the program ends.

The conclusion of the ROP year is a time of celebration for the entire family, ministry, church, and community. To witness the joy on the boys' faces, their shoulders squared with the pride of accomplishment for completing 33 weeks of ROP is worth it! You'll read more about the graduation ceremony in the next chapter.

Chapter 7

Graduation—Celebrating the Initiates

It's been 33 weeks of early Saturday morning drill and push-ups, Bible lessons and memory verses, uniform corrections, discipline and rewards, trips and outings, breakfast and snacks and weekly one-on-one telephone calls to realize success. Consistency and godly modeling do pay off! Finally, it's time to present these young men to their parents, extended family, church and community.

The program culminates in late October with a formal ROP graduation ceremony—a celebratory time to recognize the Initiates' hard work, determination, and perseverance. In the weeks leading up to the ceremony and graduation, we present the boys to the congregation and announce their accomplishments.

Recognition is vital! Applauding the commitment of these young men acknowledges their hard work and determination to complete the training. Publicly recognizing their collective and individual accomplishments instills godly pride for parents and sons alike. Grandparents, aunts, uncles, cousins, and friends also attend the ceremony to cheer and celebrate.

We invite former Initiates, those who have graduated from the program, to give their testimonies of what ROP has meant to them. Imagine how inspiring it is to the younger Initiates to see their peers credit ROP for helping them succeed! Graduation reinforces the enormous accomplishment of both present and past Initiates.

Program Description

The ROP Program book highlights the boys, their families, and their supporters. It's also a source of revenue because supporters and businesses purchase a one-page advertisement. We usually define the program with this brief paragraph:

> The Rites of Passage Ministry is a discipleship program designed to provide manhood training for boys ages 12-15. We adopt the African model that male elders in the village are responsible for training boys to become productive members of society by maturing in five areas—spiritual, educational, social, physical, and vocational.

The Ceremony

Everyone, including guests, is welcome to wear African attire. The ceremony begins with a lunch buffet; we presell tickets to cover the expense. During dessert, the boys receive their special awards and recognition. Over the years, we learned that keeping the official ceremony to an hour is wise. And, we schedule a rehearsal the week prior to the graduation so that the program runs smoothly.

We begin the official program with the sound of the African drums played by Elder Fred Brewer and his drummers. The boys march to their seats, buoyed by the applause of their family, friends, and congregation. Once seated, there's prayer and a song by our guest singer. The Chairman introduces himself, and each elder follows with a brief description of his role in the program. A script of the Graduation Ceremony is in Part 2.

Knowing what works and what needs to be improved has been invaluable to ROP. The Parent Council may be the best ones to survey the parents during exit interviews at the end of the program year. Following are questions we ask.

ROP PARENT SATISFACTION SURVEY

The information you provide will be reviewed and discussed by the Village Elders and Parent Council. Your feedback is invaluable to the ministry leaders. The information you share with us will be used to benefit the current year and future Rites of Passage programs. Thank you in advance for your participation in this process.

1. Has there been a positive change noticed in your son since the start of the program? ❑ Yes ❑ No

    Please explain your answer.

2. What area of the ministry are you most pleased with?

3. What is one area you would like to see changed to strengthen the ROP Program?

4. What would you like to see added to enhance future ROP programs?

5. **Please use the scale below to rate the following components of the ROP program.**

	Poor			Average				Excellent		
Education……………..	1	2	3	4	5	6	7	8	9	10
Social…………………	1	2	3	4	5	6	7	8	9	10
Spiritual………………	1	2	3	4	5	6	7	8	9	10
Physical………………	1	2	3	4	5	6	7	8	9	10
Vocational……………	1	2	3	4	5	6	7	8	9	10
Outings………………	1	2	3	4	5	6	7	8	9	10
Parent Meetings………	1	2	3	4	5	6	7	8	9	10
Village Elders…………	1	2	3	4	5	6	7	8	9	10
Champions……………	1	2	3	4	5	6	7	8	9	10
Parent Council……….	1	2	3	4	5	6	7	8	9	10
Parent Team Training…	1	2	3	4	5	6	7	8	9	10
Special Events…………	1	2	3	4	5	6	7	8	9	10

(i.e. Mother's Day, Men's Appreciation Day, etc.)

Parents please indicate a rating of your support of the ROP ministry	1	2	3	4	5	6	7	8	9	10

Please use the space below to write any additional comments you may have:

Chapter 8

Question—When Should You Begin?

Pray. Get a few good men and mothers to join you. And step out of the boat into the water. The Lord will sustain you, provide for you, and guide you. Start small, like we did with one boy. Or start with a couple of boys. Be sure to have one Champion per boy or Initiate.

To some, the word "mentor" may sound overwhelming. Use a term like "Champion," and stress that the commitment only lasts during the program year, not a lifetime.

Be consistent. God will send like-minded, Holy Spirit-filled volunteers.

Begin now! Your theme may be military (like ours). Or you may have a sports theme, drill team, arts, or business/entrepreneurial theme. Choose what works best for your setting. Be creative. Programs should comprise these five principles: spiritual, educational, social, vocational, and physical.

Remember

Be consistent. If leaders step out of line, they should be held accountable. The Chairman may set up a meeting to discuss the offense. When necessary, we recommend counseling or an appointment with the pastoral advisor.

Your Reward

God will reward your gift of time and resources in ways you can't imagine. Trust Him! He sees your dedication and commitment to excellence and your hours of prayer and preparation. Let this promise propel you forward:

> God is not unjust; he will not forget your work and the love you have shown him
> as you have helped his people and continue to help them. (Hebrews 6:10, NIV)

Begin now. Begin with a small team. Begin with one or two boys. But begin! Take the first year to plan and recruit, which is well worth the effort. Hopefully, this book answers many questions you must address as you plan.

Be creative. Be courageous. We are praying with you and for you!

_____

I am committing to begin a Rites of Passage Ministry in my church. Holy Spirit, please guide me! In Jesus' name, I pray, Amen.

_____

Name

_____

Date

_____

Part 2

Forms and Worksheets

On the following pages are examples of forms and worksheets to be reviewed, approved, and modified by your church's legal counsel for your ROP program. These forms are worksheets that serve as suggestions of the type of information you may need for your program. In no way are the following forms and worksheets to be considered as definitive official documents.

1. First Meeting Agenda (2015)
2. Parent/Guardian Information Package
   a. Information Sheet
   b. 2021 Calendar Year
   c. Youth and Parent/Guardian Application
   d. Parent/Guardian Information
   e. Medical History of Initiate
   f. Participation Permission Slip
   g. Parent/Guardian Confidentiality Statement
   h. Parent Signature Page/Ministry Use Only
   i. Authorization to Pick Up My Son
   j. Disciplinary Procedures
   k. Rewards and Recognitions
   l. Attendance Policy
   m. Sexual Abstinence Permission Slip
   n. Uniform Code Policy
   o. Visual/Audio Image Release Form
   p. Parent Commitment Statement
   q. Initiate T-Shirt Order Form
   r. FAX Transmittal
3. Champion Application
   a. Champion Interview Questions
   b. Marks of an ROP Champion
   c. 10 Ways Champions Win
   d. Some Do's of Champion Mentoring
   e. Some Don'ts of Champion Mentoring
4. Fundraiser Package
5. Graduation Ceremony Storyboard with Pledges

Feel free to reproduce the ROP logo, which is specifically designed for this book.

First Meeting Agenda

RITES OF PASSAGE
December 16, 2015
Elder Irving H. Tolbert, Chairman

Opening Prayer
Overview of Meeting Objective
Outline of Key Components

-Recruiting Men/Boys
    Fund Raising
    Media

-Utilization Professional Counseling
    Help Identify Potential Mental Issues
    Parental Training Aids
    Ministry Leadership Training Aids
    21st Century Family Interface
    Help Develop Behavioral Guidelines
    Help Develop Intake Guidelines/Identify Red Flags

-Intake Processes
    Vet Parents/Expectations/Commitment/Involvement/Reinforcement
    Vet Initiate/What We Expect/Goal of Training/Behavioral Red Flags
    Vet Champions/What we Expect/Our Commitment Goal

-Class Room Structure/Teachers Training
    Teacher Training
    Age-Appropriate Curriculum
    Structured Lessons and Classroom Setting
    Create Specific ROP Curriculum
    Identify Teachers For The Program Year

-Program Year Calendar/Behavior Policy
    Build On Established Behavior Policy
    Establish Misbehavior Tolerance Maximums
    Establish A Strict Program Calendar
    Establish Drill Criteria/Expectations/Behavior Guidelines

Choose Your Team (At Least Two Different Village Elders/MOV on each team)

RITES OF PASSAGE

ROP Information Package

Rites of Passage
Information Sheet

Rites of Passage is a ministry of _____Church that runs an annual program for boys aged 12-15. The ministry helps boys transition into godly manhood. The program averages 33 weeks or eight months and occurs on Saturday mornings from 7am to 11am.

Village Elders lead the Rites of Passage program and are supported by Champions, Instructors and the Parent Council. Physical training and instructors teach discipline, train and test the Initiates (boys) in particular subjects such as Bible study, health, hygiene, and sexuality, sexual abstinence and life skills, social skills, goal setting, First Aid, and more.

Every month, there are opportunities for recreational and educational field trips or activities. Activities include: hiking, camping, going to Catalina Island, Jet Propulsion Laboratories, Union Rescue Mission, visiting the African-American Firefighters' museum, community service, and a college tour.

Each boy (Initiate) is assigned to teams, which include Village Elders and Champions. Each Champion is assigned one or two Initiates. Champions complete training sessions, pass an interview and background check, and commit to spending time supporting and encouraging the Initiates throughout the program year.

Parents commit to drop-off and pick-up their Initiate on time each week (6:45 am and 11:00 am) to attend monthly parental meetings, and to support the program by volunteering each month to assist with administrative duties.

THE SCHEDULE AND CURRICULUM

6:45-7:00am PROGRAM SIGN-IN

7am-8:45am PHYSICAL TRAINING

9am-11am CLASSROOM INSTRUCTION - one hour classes that cover:

- o Spiritual growth (Bible Study)
- o Educational growth (School subject skills)
- o Physical growth (Health, Hygiene, and Sexuality)
- o Social growth (Sexual Abstinence and Life Skills)
- o Vocational Skills (Auto/Home Maintenance)

INITIAL REQUIREMENTS FOR INITIATES AND PARENTS/GUARDIANS
- o Attend the mandatory orientation.
- o Submit a completed application and attend an interview session.
- o Parent(s) and Initiate both must attend the orientation and interview.
- o Pay $100.00 initial fee (one-time fee).

REQUIREMENTS FOR CHAMPIONS:
Bring your knowledge, life experience, wisdom, and skills to help change and impact the lives of our boys. Come and be part of a positive solution by giving back to your community and changing someone's life at the same time.

FOR ADDITIONAL INFORMATION, CONTACT US:
Phone:
Email:
Website:
Facebook:
Instagram:

RITES OF PASSAGE

<table>
<tr><td>Prayer Call: Every 1st & 3rd Thursday</td></tr>
</table>

Rites of Passage 2021 Calendar Year

All Dates are Tentative. Dates in red represent no ROP.   **Draft February 17, 2021**

January

Sun	Mon	Tues	Wed	Thur	Fri	Sat
					1	2
3	4	5	6	7	8	9
10	11	12	13	14	15	16
17	18	19	20	21	22	23
24	25	26	27	28	29	30
31						

February

Sun	Mon	Tues	Wed	Thur	Fri	Sat
	1	2	3	4	5	6
7	8	9	10	11	12	13
14	15	16	17	18	19	20
21	22	23	24	25	26	27
28						

March

Sun	Mon	Tues	Wed	Thur	Fri	Sat
	1	2	3	4	5	6
7	8	9	10	11	12	13
14	15	16	17	18	19	20
21	22	23	24	25	26	27
28	29	30	31			
7:30 Mandatory Parent Meeting

April

Sun	Mon	Tues	Wed	Thur	Fri	Sat
				1	2	3
4	5	6	7	8	9	10
11	12	13	14	15	16	17
18	19	20	21	22	23	24
25	26	27	28	29	30	
7:30 Mandatory Parent Meeting

May

Sun	Mon	Tues	Wed	Thur	Fri	Sat
						1
2	3	4	5	6	7	8
9	10	11	12	13	14	15
16	17	18	19	20	21	22
23	24	25	26	27	28	29
30	31	7:30 Mandatory Parent Meeting

June

Sun	Mon	Tues	Wed	Thur	Fri	Sat
		1	2	3	4	5
6	7	8	9	10	11	12
13	14	15	16	17	18	19
20	21	22	23	24	25	26
27	28	29	30			
7:30 Mandatory Parent Meeting

July

Sun	Mon	Tues	Wed	Thur	Fri	Sat
Souvenir Book Kick-Off				1	2	3
4	5	6	7	8	9	10
11	12	13	14	15	16	17
18	19	20	21	22	23	24
25	26	27	28	29	30	31
7:30 Mandatory Parent Meeting

August

Sun	Mon	Tues	Wed	Thur	Fri	Sat
1	2	3	4	5	6	7
8	9	10	11	12	13	14
15	16	17	18	19	20	21
22	23	24	25	26	27	28
29	30	30				
30	31	7:30 Mandatory Parent Meeting

September

Sun	Mon	Tues	Wed	Thur	Fri	Sat
			1	2	2	4
5	6	7	8	9	10	11
12	13	14	15	16	17	18
19	20	21	22	23	24	25
26	27	28	28	30		
7:30 Mandatory Parent Meeting

October

Sun	Mon	Tues	Wed	Thur	Fri	Sat
					1	2
3	4	5	6	7	8	9
10	11	12	13	14	15	16
17	18	19	20	21	22	23
24	25	26	27	28	29	30
31						

November

Sun	Mon	Tues	Wed	Thur	Fri	Sat
	1	2	3	4	5	6
7	8	9	10	11	12	13
14	15	16	17	18	19	20
21	22	23	24	25	26	27
28	29	30				

December

Sun	Mon	Tues	Wed	Thur	Fri	Sat
			1	2	2	4
5	6	7	8	9	10	11
12	13	14	15	16	17	18
19	20	21	22	23	24	25
26	27	28	28	30	31	

Events

January
Jan 1 — New Year's Day
Jan 15 — Martin Luther King Birthday
Jan 18 — Martin Luther King Holiday

February
Feb 15 — President's Day

March
Mar 6 — ROP Orientation
Mar 13 — 1st Program Day 7:00 – 11:00 am
Mar 13 — Parent Meet & Greet
Mar 13 — Champion Training - 8:00 am
Mar 20 — Prayer Meeting – 7:30 am
Mar 20 — Champion Training - 8:00 am
Mar 27 — Mandatory Parent Meeting
Mar 27 — Champion Training - 8:00 am

April
Apr 4 — Easter
Apr 17 — Prayer Meeting – 7:30 am
Apr 24 — Mandatory Parent Meeting

May
May 8 — Mother's Day Luncheon
May 9 — Mother's Day
May 15 — End of Phase 1
May 15 — Prayer Meeting - 7:30 am
May 22 — Mandatory Parent Meeting
May 29 — No ROP: Holiday Weekend
May 31 — Memorial Day

June
Jun 19 — Prayer Meeting - 7:30 am
Jun — Compton Courthouse
Jun 26 — Mandatory Parent Meeting

July
Jul 3 — No ROP: Holiday Weekend
Jul 4 — Independence Day.
Jul 17 — Prayer Meeting - 7:30 am
Jul 24 — Mandatory Parent Meeting
NOTE: The Souvenir Book Fundraiser will Kick-Off This Month

August
Aug 7 — ROP Picnic
Aug 14 — End of Phase 2
Aug 21 — Prayer Meeting - 7:30 am
Aug 28 — Mandatory Parent Meeting

September
Sep 4 — No ROP Labor Day Wkend
Sep 6 — Labor Day
Sep 18 — Prayer Meeting - 7:30 am
Sep 25 — Mandatory Parent Meeting
Sep 25 — Pass and Review

October
Oct 9 — Graduation Rehearsal
Oct 16 — Graduation Rehearsal
Oct 23 — Banquet/Ceremony
Oct 30 — Trunk or Treat

November
Nov 11 — Veterans Day
Nov — Boxes of Love
Nov 25 — Thanksgiving Day

December
Dec 11 — Angel Tree
Dec 25 — Christmas Day

RITES OF PASSAGE

ROP

RITES OF PASSAGE

Nurturing boys into godly men
by developing the qualities they need for successful manhood

YOUTH AND PARENT/GUARDIAN APPLICATION

Return the completed application using one of the following methods:
1. Email the completed application to
2. Fill out online at https://www._____
3. Fax the application. Use the enclosed fax cover sheet printed on "Page 6" of this application.

☐ **PLEASE PRINT ALL INFORMATION**
* This section must be completed by the initiate *

_____   _____   _____
Initiate's First Name   Middle Name   Last Name

_____   _____   _____   _____
Age   Date of Birth   Name of the school you attend   Grade Level

Names and ages of your brothers: _____

_____

Names and ages of your sisters: _____

_____

_____   _____
What letter grades do you receive?   What is your favorite subject?

_____   _____
What are your hobbies?   What do you want to be when you grow up?

_____   _____
Name of your role model?   How much time do you spend with him?

Describe what makes you happy: _____

_____

Describe what makes you angry: _____

_____

Describe what makes you sad: _____

_____

Have you accepted Christ as your Lord and Savior? ☐ Yes   ☐ No

How do you know you are saved?   _____

_____

_____

RITES OF PASSAGE

ROP

RITES OF PASSAGE
Nurturing boys into godly men
by developing the qualities they need for successful manhood

PARENT/GUARDIAN INFORMATION

Initiate _____

Parent(s)/Guardian(s) _____ & _____

☐ **PLEASE ANSWER ALL QUESTIONS**

PLEASE MARK ONE: ☐ **Parent**   ☐ **Guardian**

First Name	Middle Name	Last Name
Street Address	City/ State	Zip Code
Home Phone	Cell Phone	Work Phone	Fax No
Primary Email Address	Alternate Email Address
Emergency Contact: Name	Phone No.	Relationship

☐ Married ☐ Single ☐ Divorced   _____   _____
Birth Date (Month/Day)   Number of Children

_____
What Church Do You Attend? How Long?

Does father play an active role in the initiate's life?   ☐ Yes   ☐ No

Does mother play an active role in the initiate's life?   ☐ Yes   ☐ No

How did you hear about the ROP Program? _____

_____

_____

Why do you want your son involved with the ROP Program? _____

_____

_____

_____

_____

_____

_____

RITES OF PASSAGE

MEDICAL HISTORY OF INITIATE

INJURIES

Broken or Cracked Bones……………………………………..….… No ☐ Yes ☐

Sprains…………………………………………………….……..….… No ☐ Yes ☐

Lacerations……………………………………………………........ No ☐ Yes ☐

Dislocations……………………………………………………….… No ☐ Yes ☐

Concussion or Head Injury…………………………………….… No ☐ Yes ☐

Ever Been Knocked Unconscious………………………………… No ☐ Yes ☐

If yes to any of the above, please explain below

_____

_____

YOUR SON'S PAST SURGICAL HISTORY:

Appendectomy…………………………………………………….… No ☐ Yes ☐

Any Other Operation(s)……………………………………….…… No ☐ Yes ☐

List Other Operations(s)…………………………………………… No ☐ Yes ☐

_____

Has your son been hospitalized for any illness…………………. No ☐ Yes ☐

If yes, please explain below

_____

_____

CURRENT MEDICAL STATUS OF YOUR SON:

Son's Current Weight:_____ Son's Current Height _____
Son's Current Allergies: _____

List all current medications your son takes (prescription and non-prescription)

_____

_____

Does your son wear glasses………………………………………………….. No ☐ Yes ☐
(When were his eyes last checked_____/_____/_____)

When was your son's last physical_____/_____/_____

RITES OF PASSAGE

PARTICIPATION PERMISSION SLIP

I_____ give my permission to_____,
(Please Circle one: Parent or Legal Guardian)   (Initiate)
a minor, to participate in this program and all activities thereof.

This interaction will commence _____ and will end approximately 33 weeks later

on _____.

I acknowledge that Rites of Passage has the authority of the following dates stated above:

☐   To consent to any medical treatment that may be required by in the place and with the same authority as PARENT.

☐   Further, in consideration of the services performed by the employees, elders, champions, volunteers and agents of _____ Church and the Rites of Passage are herewith released from liability for all actions taken in good faith during the program.

Dated:_____/_____/_____

_____
Printed Name of PARENT

_____
Signature of PARENT

RITES OF PASSAGE

ROP

RITES OF PASSAGE

Nurturing boys into godly men
by developing the qualities they need for successful manhood

PARENT / GUARDIAN CONFIDENTIALITY STATEMENT

The information you provide in this section will be held in the strictest of confidence.

To better serve and minister to your initiate, please answer the following questions as thoroughly as possible.

Initiate _____

Parent(s)/Guardian(s)_____ & _____

1. Has your child been subject to, or involved with the following:

     a.   A Therapist?   No ☐   Yes ☐

     b.   Anger, fits of rage?   No ☐   Yes ☐

     c.   Emotional outburst?   No ☐   Yes ☐

     d.   Aggressive or violent behavior?   No ☐   Yes ☐

     e.   Destructive behavior?   No ☐   Yes ☐

     f.   Drugs or alcohol use?   No ☐   Yes ☐

     g.   Gang related activity?   No ☐   Yes ☐

     h.   Self injury?   No ☐   Yes ☐

     i.   Psychotic episodes?   No ☐   Yes ☐

     j.   Matters related to juvenile court system or the police department? No ☐   Yes ☐

If you answered yes, to any of the above questions, please provide a detailed explanation.

_____

_____

_____

_____

2. Has your son been suspended or expelled from school in the past 2 years? No ☐ Yes ☐

If your answer is yes, please provide a detailed explanation. _____

_____

_____

_____

_____

3. Please place an X below to identify the description which best describes your son.

     a.   ☐   Mild mannered

     b.   ☐   Compliant

     c.   ☐   Strong willed

     d.   ☐   Angry

     e.   ☐   Depressed

     f.   ☐   Aggressive

     g.   ☐   Lacks confidence

     h.   ☐   Anti-Social (common disregard for social rules, norms, and cultural codes, as well as impulsive behavior, and indifference to the rights and feelings of others)

RITES OF PASSAGE

PARENT / GUARDIAN CONFIDENTIALITY STATEMENT

(Continued)

Initiate _____

Parent(s)/Guardian(s)_____ & _____

4. How would you rate your son's respect for authority? Please place an X below.
   a. ☐ High degree of respect for authority
   b. ☐ Some respect for authority
   c. ☐ No respect for authority

5. Has your son been subject to psychological, sexual or physical abuse? ☐ No ☐ Yes

__ **ADDITIONAL SPACE FOR COMMENTS** *(Please use a separate sheet of paper if more space is needed):* __

Comments:

RITES OF PASSAGE

YOUTH AND PARENT/GUARDIAN APPLICATION

Initiate _____

Your signature acknowledges that the information you have provided in this application is true and correct to the best of your knowledge.

_____   _____
Parent / Guardian   Date

_____   _____
Parent / Guardian   Date

FOR MINISTRY USE ONLY	
Date of Interview:	Interviewed by:
Comments:	

RITES OF PASSAGE

AUTHORIZATION TO PICK UP MY SON

I,_____, the parent or legal guardian of
       (printed name of parent/guardian)

_____, a minor, do hereby authorize the following
       (printed name of minor)

Person(s) to pick up my son from activities conducted by the Rites of Passage:

_____   _____
Printed Name   *Relationship*

(_____)_____
Telephone Number

_____   _____
Printed Name   *Relationship*

(_____)_____
Telephone Number

_____   _____
Printed Name   *Relationship*

(_____)_____
Telephone Number

This authorization shall remain in effect as long as my son participates in programs sponsored by the Rites of Passage. I understand that it is solely the responsibility of the parent/guardian to notify the Rites of Passage, in writing, of any changes to those persons authorized to pick up my son.

_____   _____
Printed Name of Parent/Guardian   *Signature of Parent/Guardian   DATE*

DISCIPLINARY PROCEDURES

1. To assist the student in meeting ROP's Standard of Conduct, two offenses, general and major offenses, have been established.

When it is reasonably established that a student has committed an offense or violation of ROP regulation, appropriate disciplinary action will be taken. The nature and frequency of the violation will determine the severity of the discipline.

At the discretion of the ROP Board of Elders, informal verbal counseling may occur prior to the issuance of formal discipline. These communications are intended to create an open, problem-solving environment between the student and ROP.

ROP's formal disciplinary policy is progressive and cumulative; committing successive offenses whether general or major will result in the next step of discipline.

GENERAL OFFENSE

a. Disruptive behavior - gestures, noises, and irregular movements that will interfere with the learning environment
b. Horseplay – of any kind at any time will not be acceptable
c. Creating discord or lack of harmony by actions such as ridicule, teasing, and name calling, etc.
d. Cursing or swearing

DISCIPLINARY PROCEDURES

(1) Verbal Warnings
(2) Detention – the severity of the detention is at the discretion of the drill instructors

MAJOR OFFENSE

e. Insubordination

RITES OF PASSAGE

      (1) Willful disobedience of any reasonable and legitimate instructions issued by any member of ROP Staff

      (2) Addressing such person/s in an abusive, threatening, or contemptuous manner

         (a) Defacing church property

f. Theft and unauthorized removal of property belonging to another

g. Committing any act of violence

h. Introduction or possession of illegal substances or weapons

      (1) Parent conference

      (2) Dismissal

RITES OF PASSAGE

REWARDS AND RECOGNITION

In order to encourage good behavior students will be recognized and awards will be distributed as determined by the ROP Elder Board.

Some of the rewards as follows:

(1) Certificate recognizing Outstanding Behavior
(2) Certificate recognizing Perfect Attendance
(3) Promotions to positions of responsibility (Squad Leader)
(4) Gift Certificates
(5) Recognition in the monthly Newsletter
(6) Other rewards to be determined by ROP Elder Board

I have read and understood the Rites of Passage Discipline Procedures, and I agree to follow the rules and guidelines set forth by the ROP Ministry.

[Print] Initiate Name	Initiate Signature	Date
[Print] Parent / Guardian Name	Parent / Guardian Signature	Date
[Print] ROP/Elder	ROP/Elder Signature	Date
[Print] Parent Council	Parent Council Signature	Date

RITES OF PASSAGE

ATTENDANCE POLICY

Saturday drill and classroom attendance is mandatory! In order to graduate from the ROP program and actively participate in the October Graduation Ceremony, an Initiate must be committed. There are approximately 33 program Saturdays, including one of the two graduation rehearsals. Failure to attend at least 30 Saturdays will disqualify an Initiate from graduating. Missing outings is considered an absence. If the Initiate is disqualified from the program, he may attend the graduation as a invited guest.

_____   _____   _____
[Print] Initiate Name   Initiate Signature   Date

_____   _____   _____
[Print] Parent / Guardian Name Parent / Guardian Signature   Date

_____   _____   _____
[Print] ROP/Elder   ROP/Elder Signature   Date

_____   _____   _____
[Print] Parent Council   Parent Council Signature   Date

RITES OF PASSAGE

SEXUAL ABSTINENCE PERMISSION SLIP

Dear Parent / Guardian,

We are pleased to inform you that we will be teaching a six-week curriculum designed to encourage your son to choose abstinence until marriage. The program will consist of definitions and fundamental ideas on what it means to remain sexually abstinent in today's society. Course curriculum includes how the Holy Spirit relates to our feelings and emotions; exposing the allurements and distractions of the enemy; sexual harassment training; spiritual influence of Hip Hop music/videos; fun, games, and prizes. The goal is to empower teenagers to develop effective decision-making skills that help them choose abstinence by affirming "Not Yet" or "No More."

You are encouraged to contact the Program Director to arrange a time to preview the lessons or ask questions about the program. Homework assignments will be given and your cooperation and participation is encouraged. You are an important part of helping to shape the values in the lives of your children, which will be good enough to last a lifetime. In order to help your son make right decisions it is very important to have discussions with him about these lessons.

Please sign the bottom of this form allowing your son permission to participate in this exciting curriculum. If you have any questions, please do not hesitate to call. Thank you in advance for helping this course an educational success.

Sincerely,

ROP Chairman

_____

RITES OF PASSAGE

My son,_____has permission to participate in the Sexual Abstinence course in the Rites of Passage Program.

Signature:_____Date:
_____Parent/ Guardian

Parents/Guardians: If this form is not returned, it will be assumed that the student has permission to participate in this six-week curriculum.[12]

---

[12]   A. C. Green. (1995). *I've got the Power Abstinence Curriculum for Middle and High School Students.*

54

RITES OF PASSAGE

UNIFORM CODE POLICY

PHASE ONE

1. Grey sweats (matching) long sleeves with no emblems, logos, or writing of any kind. Just plain grey sweats. Tee shirts worn under the sweatshirt should be black or white (no exceptions).
2. Sneakers (tennis shoes) should be either black or white. They may have both colors, meaning black and white.
3. No loud or neon colors will be permitted such as purple, red, orange, green, yellow, etc.
4. No jewelry of any kind for any reason. This includes piercings.
5. Hair should be of a style and length that will allow the military and the graduation cap to be worn without any hair protruding from the sides, rear and front. We strongly urge that the hair be cut in a short style not to exceed 1/2 inch in length. Facial hair is not permitted.
6. No headgear of any kind. This includes bandanas, caps, "hoodies", scarves, etc.
7. No gloves.
8. No eyewear except for those with a written prescription. Parents must provide a copy of the doctor's recommendation for dark colored glasses.

PHASE TWO

1. The standard camouflaged fatigues as prescribed by the staff must be worn in a military fashion. It must be clean and pressed at all times.
2. The boots also prescribed by the staff, must be clean and polished at all times.
3. The drill instructors will conduct a training session in advance to explain how to wear the uniform.
4. No modifications of the uniform will be allowed.

RITES OF PASSAGE

PARENT / INITIATE AGREEMENT

I have received, read and agree to the dress code established by the staff. I understand that these terms are non-negotiable.

Date:_____

Initiate's Signature:_____Print:_____

Parent's Signature:_____Print: _____

Parent's Signature:_____Print: _____

RITES OF PASSAGE

VISUAL/AUDIO IMAGE RELEASE FORM

I grant permission to _____ Church, Rites of Passage Ministry (ROP), its employees and agents, to take and use visual/audio images of me and my son as participants of the program. Visual/audio images are any type of recording, including but not limited to photographs, digital images, drawings, renderings, voices, sounds, video recordings, audio clips or accompanying written descriptions. ROP will not materially alter the original images. I agree that ROP owns the images and all rights related to them. The images may be used in any manner or media without notifying me, such as church sponsored websites, publications, promotions, broadcasts, advertisements, posters and theater slides, as well as for non-church uses. I waive any right to inspect or approve the finished images or any printed or electronic matter that may be used with them, or to be compensated for them.

I release ROP and its employees and agents, including any firm authorized to publish, broadcast and/or distribute a finished product containing the images, from any claims, damages or liability which I may ever have in connection with the taking or use of the images or printed material used with the images. I am at least 18 years of age and competent to sign this release. I have read this release before signing, I understand its contents, meaning and impact, and I freely accept the terms.

_____   _____
Initiate's Signature   [Print] Initiate's Name

_____   _____   _____
Parent / Guardian Signature   Print Name   Date

_____   _____   _____
Parent / Guardian Signature   Print Name   Date

RITES OF PASSAGE

PARENT COMMITMENT STATEMENT

It Takes A Village To Raise A Child

1. I will sign-in my son on Saturdays at 6:45 am.
2. I will arrive prior to 11:00 am on Saturdays to sign-out my son.
3. I will attend Mandatory Parent Meetings on 4th Saturdays from 7:30 – 9:30 am.
4. I will volunteer once a month to support my designated parent team from 6:30 am – 12:30 pm.
5. I will read and confirm receipt of the ROP Weekly Letters and all emailed correspondence.
6. I will partner with the ROP ministry team and assist wherever I can to help during this journey of the Lord nurturing boys into godly young men.

Please indicate here if for some reason you cannot meet this obligation. If so, a meeting will be scheduled with you, a Village Elder, and a Parent Council member.

Reason:_____

_____
[Print] Initiate's Name

_____	_____	_____
[Print] Parent / Guardian Name	Parent / Guardian Signature	Date
_____	_____	_____
[Print] ROP Elder	ROP Elder Signature	Date
_____	_____	_____
[Print] Parent Council	Parent Council Signature	Date

RITES OF PASSAGE

Initiate T-Shirt Order Form

Greetings Parents,

The Rites of Passage Ministry will provide a t-shirt for your initiate to wear on program outings. Please provide the information below for your son to assist us with placing the order.

Date:_____

Initiate's Name:_____

Form Completed by:_____

Relationship to Initiate:

Parent   Guardian   Other_____

* *

Initiate's T-Shirt Size:

* * * *Please note, only men size t-shirts will be ordered * * * *

Small   Medium   Large   XL   XXL

RITES OF PASSAGE

ROP

RITES OF PASSAGE

Nurturing boys into godly men
by developing the qualities they need for successful manhood

FAX TRANSMITTAL

If application is being faxed, please use this cover sheet

Date	
Sent by	
Phone #	
Faxed To	ATTENTION : RITES OF PASSAGE MINISTRY
Subject	
Total # Pages	

MESSAGE:

RITES OF PASSAGE

CHAMPION APPLICATION

Date_____

☞ **PLEASE PRINT ALL INFORMATION**

First Name   Middle Name   Last Name

Street Address (P.O. Boxes are not accepted)

_____

City   State   Zip Code

_____

Home Phone   Email Address

_____

Cell Phone   Fax Number

MARITAL STATUS (Please Check One):   Married [ ] Divorced [ ]   Widowed [ ] Single [ ]

Number of Children (if any)_____

Are you a member of _____? Y_____/ N_____

If you answered yes to being a member then are you actively engaged in ministry? Y___/ N___

Ministry Name (if applicable)_____

We are primarily a Saturday based ministry. Are you available on that day? Y_____/ N_____

Please continue on the next page ➴

RITES OF PASSAGE

In the space provided below, please briefly describe your reason for wanting to be involved with Rites of Passage and any factors you believe prepare you to serve in this area of ministry.

_____

_____

_____

_____

_____

_____

_____

_____

Personal Information

It is the goal of ROP to create a safe and secure atmosphere for all children who participate in activities of this church. To facilitate that purpose, it is necessary to gather certain information from individuals desiring to interact with children and youth. This information will be used for the sole purpose of helping the church provide a safe and secure environment for those children who participate in our program and use our facilities.

Other name(s) you have been known by (if any):

Date of Birth: Social Security No:

CA Driver's License: Marital Status:

RITES OF PASSAGE

References

List three references that are not related to you by birth or marriage. References that know of your work with youth or children in a mentoring capacity are preferable. At least one reference must be a church member.

	Reference 1	Reference 2	Reference 3
Name			
Title/Position			
Address			
Organization			
Telephone: daytime & evening (if available)			
How long have you known this person?			
Office Use Only:			

Church History

1. List all churches you were a member of or attended on a regular basis in the past 5 years:

   _____

   _____

2. Have you ever been a child/youth worker, instructor or volunteer before? ☐ Yes ☐ No

   If yes, when and in what capacity?_____

   _____

3. Do you have any training/certification in first aid or CPR? ☐ Yes ☐ No

Please continue on the next page ⤳

RITES OF PASSAGE

Background

We believe it is our responsibility to seek adult volunteers that are able to provide healthy, safe and nurturing environments. In order to accomplish this, we need to ask some personal questions that may be uncomfortable to answer. If you prefer, you may discuss your answers in confidence with a pastor rather than answering on this form. All applications are kept confidential.

1. Is there any circumstance that might call into question your being entrusted to work with or be in contact with children or youth?

    Yes ☐   No ☐
    Please comment:

2. Do you have any concerns about working with children or youth? Yes ☐   No ☐

    Please comment:

3. Have you ever participated in, been accused or convicted or pleaded guilty or no contest to any abuse or sexual misconduct, sexual harassment, or other immoral behavior or conduct involving children, youth or adults?

    Yes ☐   No ☐

    Please comment:

    _____

    _____

    _____

    _____

    _____

Confidential Information

I certify that all information on this application is true to the best of my knowledge. I understand that any false statements or withheld information will be reason to disqualify me from serving as a ROP Volunteer.

I give my permission to the church volunteers/staff of this program to contact the references listed above. I also understand that a criminal background check will be conducted. Furthermore, I authorize the volunteers/staff to inquire about my previous/present volunteer and work experience.

All information obtained will be treated confidentially and will not be disclosed to others outside the volunteers/staff immediately involved in the ministry screening process unless the staff determines that disclosure is necessary for the protection of the church.

I have read and understand a background check will be conducted.

Signature:_____

This application must be signed and dated to be processed.

_____   _____
         Applicant Signature   Date

FOR MINISTRY USE ONLY

Date of 1st Interview ____/____/____

Date of background check ____/____/____   Application accepted [ ]   Rejected [ ]

Date of orientation ____/____/____

Name of initiate assigned _____

RITES OF PASSAGE

Champion Interview Questions

1. **Introductions/Open with Prayer**

2. **Review the vision of the Rites of Passage ministry**

   "The vision of the Rites of Passage ministry is to equip boys for their passage into godly manhood by encouraging them to grow spiritually, physically, educationally, vocationally, and socially through the biblically based, annual program run by the village elders and the champions."

   The following questions are based on various areas of the vision of ROP.

3. **Spiritual growth**
   - What is your current ministry involvement at _____?
   - Tell us about your walk with the Lord? (strengths/weaknesses)
   - Do you believe that adultery is a sin?
   - Do you believe that fornication is a sin?
   - Do you believe that pedophilia is a sin?
   - Do you believe that homosexuality is a sin?
   - How much time do you spend daily in prayer?
   - How much time do you spend daily reading Scripture?

4. **Physical background**
   - Do you have any athletic experience (training, martial arts, and organized sports)?
   - Do you have any military experience?

5. **Educational background**
   - Tell us about your educational accomplishments.

6. **Vocational background**
   - Tell us about your career and your career goals.

7. **Social background**
   - Do you have experience working with children?

RITES OF PASSAGE

- Tell us about your family.
- Tell us about your social outlets, recreations, hobbies.

8. **Mentorship background**
   - Who was your role model in your youth?
   - What Christian man can you go to with your personal issues?
   - What are some of the attributes a good mentor should possess?
   - What motivated you to become a part of this program?

9. **Time commitment (about 2-4 hours a week)**
   - Will you spend 1 hour each week to call an Initiate?
   - Will you commit to the 4 sessions of training, 2hrs/week?
   - Will you commit to at least 3 hrs a month to support classroom instruction?

10. **Close with prayer**

Marks of an ROP Champion (Mentor)

Rites of Passage Champions serve as mentors to the boys or Initiates during the program year.

A. A mentor must have what the Initiate needs.
  1. Initiates need mentors who help them mature and grow.
  2. Be authentic. Impart to the Initiate what you know to be accurate based on your experiences or observations.
  3. A mentor must have the goods, not just the good looks. Be disciplined about your spiritual growth to have substance to contribute beyond your appearance or uniform.

B. A mentor cultivates relationships.
  1. An effective mentor must be willing to share about his life in developmentally appropriate ways.
  2. A mentor is committed to his Initiates' growth and life goals.
  3. A mentor can cultivate and maintain a relationship with the Initiate during the program year.

C. A mentor is willing to take a chance.
  1. A mentor must be willing to invest in his Initiate.
  2. This investment must include time, energy, emotion, trust, and other resources.
  3. An investment always involves a risk.
    a. Initiates may respond differently than you believe they should.
    b. Not all your mentoring efforts will appear successful; leave the results to God!

D. A mentor respects others and is respected.
  1. One crucial way to determine if a man is reliable enough to become a mentor is by his testimony (2 Tim. 2:2). What is his reputation at home, church, and community?
  2. Mentors are open letters. They are transparent, allowing others to see who they really are.

E. A mentor has a network of resources.
  As a mentor, you can help your Initiate reach his spiritual and vocational goals because of who you are—your person, character, integrity, and accomplishments—what you know, who you know, and how you live.

F. A mentor is a reliable consultant/advisor.
    1. One of the best indications that a man can serve as a guide is if he is already a successful guide to others.
    2. A mentor must recognize that not wisdom alone qualifies him to lead a young man. Wisdom applied makes the difference.
    3. A mentor must recognize that the ability to communicate well makes a difference in the Initiate's life.

G. A mentor talks *and* listens.
    1. A mentor will become an effective communicator by becoming an effective listener.
    2. Communication is a two-way street.

H. A mentor is consistent in his lifestyle.
    No one respects a man who can talk a good game but who lacks discipline. No one respects a man who does not follow or play by the rules.

I. A mentor can assess and diagnose his initiative's needs.
    A mentor must see something wrong and figure out what he or someone else can do to help, fix, or meet the need.

J. A mentor is concerned with the interest of his Initiate.
    A mentor sacrifices his personal agenda to help his Initiate grow in his Christian life, family and social relationships, and vocational life.

10 Ways Champions Wim

Young boys are tired of the same thing. They expect a relationship with a purpose that helps them meet their needs and accomplish their goals.

1. Get on your Initiate's turf.
2. Invite him onto your turf.
3. Take on a (not the) responsibility to help your initiative succeed.
4. Go through a process of overtime (extending yourself).
5. Do spiritual and recreational activities with others (never one-on-one to protect yourself, your Initiate, this ministry, and the church from allegations of sexual abuse).
6. Pray and study the Bible together during weekly calls.
7. Involve the Initiate in a project.
8. Remember, you are to help this child grow in Christ and progress toward his life goals.
9. Find something to laugh about, but not about the Initiate's looks, behavior, or personality.
10. Discuss what's going on in the world of sports or the arts. Laugh about that!

Some Do's of Champion Mentoring

1. DO follow the parents/guardians lead so that they are comfortable with your role with their son.
2. DO give the parents/guardians the ultimate respect since they are the sole authority to determine your interaction with their son.
3. DO ask the parents/guardians for the best time to call or plan activities with their son.
4. DO leave all disciplinary issues up to the parent/guardian and the Drill Sergeants.
5. DO plan occasional activities with other mentors and their Initiates. Include the Initiate's other positive male role models—fathers and grandfathers—in the activities.
6. DO establish and maintain consistent communication with parents/guardians.
7. DO maintain regular communication with the Initiate through encouragement and prayer. Discuss:
   - Integrity
   - Behavior
   - Life's humor, lessons learned, etc.
8. DO pray on the phone at the beginning of your conversation and before you hang up.
9. DO communicate to parents/guardians and the Initiate any changes in the schedule.
10. DO what you say, and say what you plan to do!

Some Don'ts of Champion Mentoring

1. Don't make plans with a boy before clearing it with his parent/guardian.
2. Don't make plans to be alone or plan a one-on-one outing with a boy; it's always the two-adult rule.
3. Don't attempt to establish a dating relationship or mingle with the parent/guardian.
4. Don't miss a commitment or fail to live up to a promise with the Initiate or his parent/guardian. In other words, don't make commitments you can't keep!
5. Don't make your only interaction an expensive outing.
6. Don't try to influence your boy's behavior too quickly. First, establish rapport and develop trust with your Initiate.
7. Don't use profanity! Profanity should never be in your vocabulary.
8. Don't use physical discipline or engage in horseplay. Leave discipline to the Drill Sergeants and the Initiate's parents or guardians.
9. Don't try to assume the role of parent/guardian.

(ROP Fundraiser Package Cover)

Celebrating 25 Years

Rites of Passage

ROP Fundraiser Package

Table of Contents

It is easier to build strong children than to repair broken men.
~ Frederick Douglass

Dear Friend and Sponsor:

The Champions for Progress ***Rites of Passage (ROP)*** is a nonprofit program for mentoring inner-city boys aged 12 to 15. We aim to help them develop valuable life skills in five areas critical to a successful life: spiritual, social, educational, physical, and vocational. Based in Inglewood, California, the program has served the community for 25 years to counsel, educate, train, and equip boys to become leaders.

Most of the initiates are African-American and Latino youth living in single-parent households without the benefit of a godly male role model. During eight intensive months (March to October), the Initiates meet weekly with volunteer mentors to learn how to develop into responsible and accountable young men of character.

Specific courses include CPR training, auto repair, health/hygiene, sexual sobriety, social/etiquette skills, first aid training, and more. Another program highlight is physical exercise, which we instill in military-style marching and calisthenics to emphasize the importance of following instructions. Recreational and educational activities include college campus tours, hiking, camping, community service, trips to Catalina Island, the Jet Propulsion Laboratories, the California Science Center, Union Rescue Mission, the African American Firefighters Museum, and the Getty Museum. The ROP mentors, instructors, and guest speakers are scientists, professors, pastors, doctors, lawyers, judges, entrepreneurs, and professional athletes who donate their time and expertise to provide the Initiates with the support and resources they need to succeed.

With your help, we can do more! The ROP budget approaches $100,000 each program year. Unfortunately, these young men's parents cannot afford the program expense, but we include everyone regardless of financial ability. Your donation will significantly impact the lives of the Initiates, their families, and the community.

To thank you for your donation, we will recognize you or your company during the various events throughout the program year. In addition, we spotlight gifts of 5,000 or more in the graduation ceremony's ***Rites of Passage*** Souvenir Book. Because extended family and friends are eager to support the youth, we average 250 to 300 attendees at this landmark celebration.

We would love to add your and your company's name to our list of supporters for all to see. Individual and corporate donations are tax-deductible. Together we can change our families, communities, and nation!

Sincerely,

Irving Tolbert

Irving Tolbert
Elder Irving Tolbert, Chairman

2023 Sponsor Opportunities Form

****

Option 1   Purchase a Sponsor Package

$7, 500 - $10,000 Marquee Sponsor	$5,000 – $7,499 Platinum Sponsor	$2,000 – $4,999 Gold Sponsor
• Two tables for 16 guests • A two-page ad in the Souvenir Sponsorship book • Recognized in Gala publicity • Listed as a Marquee Sponsor in the program	• One table for 8 guests • A two-page ad in the Souvenir Sponsorship book • Recognized in Gala publicity • Listed as a Platinum Sponsor in the program	• One table for 8 guests • A one-page ad in the Souvenir Sponsorship book • Recognized in Gala publicity • Listed as a Gold Sponsor in the program

	$ 500 – $1,999 Silver Sponso	
	• 5 tickets to the Celebration • A one-page ad in the Gala program • Recognized in Gala publicity • Listed as a Silver Sponsor in the Gala program	

Ads must be camera ready.
Please return completed forms with your ad exactly as you wish to have it printed.

Email electronic ads to:

Also email questions regarding artwork, specs or for assistance with our ad.

File format accepted.
.jpeg or .tif
Outlined or embedded fonts

If you have any questions, or require additional info, please contact:

Thank You!

Participants Name (if applicable)_____

Sponsor's Name_____

Company_____

Address/City/State/Zip_____

Phone (__)_____ Email _____

➢ TAX-DEDUCTIBLE PAYABLE TO:

➢ *FEDERAL TAX ID NUMBER:*

➢ PAYMENT METHOD:

➢ *Circle one:* VISA MASTERCARD AMER. EXPRESS CASH CHECK#_____

➢ Credit Card # _____ Exp Date _____

➢ **CREDIT CARD AUTHORIZED SIGNATURE** ➢*Please sign below*

_____

➢ _____ACBS or _____ACBM Rec'd by _____ Date _____

➢ **TOTAL PAYMENT AMOUNT RECEIVED FOR SPONSOR AD** $ _____

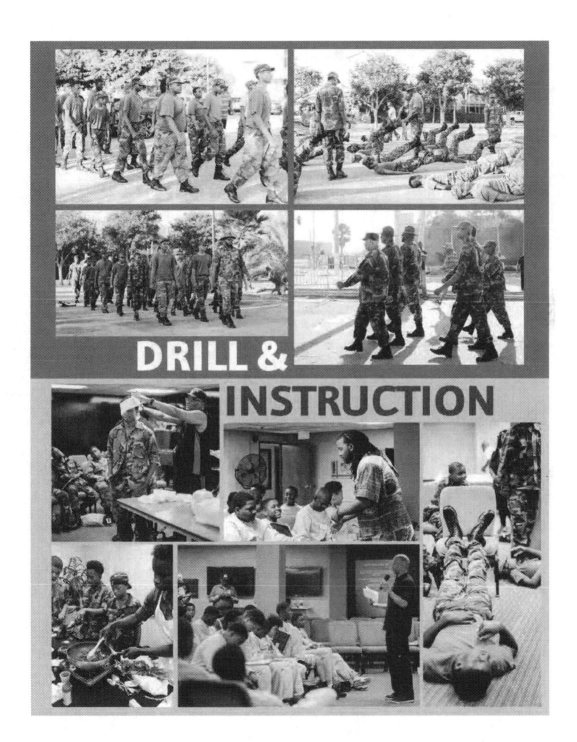

DRILL & INSTRUCTION

L.A. STADIUM PREMIERE CENTER

L.A. RAMS
TRAINING CAMP

CAMP
PENDLETON

CaliforniaScienCenter

102.3 KJLH
EMP⊙WERMENT
Summit

AHF

California State University
DOMINGUEZ HILLS
In partnership with Senator Steven Bradford

SATURDAY
9AM – 2PM
SEPTEMBER 23
CAL STATE UNIVERSITY DOMINGUEZ HILLS

Dear ROP Village Elders, MOV, Champions, Parent Council and Fellow Initiates of 2019,

I would like to submit this letter of thanks to this great ministry for all of the sacrifices made over the past 8 months. I have found myself reflecting on the lessons and events that occurred during the program year. Although the time has come to an end, I am excited about the relationships gained and the spiritual knowledge received. As I work hard to finish high school stronger than ever, I will hold on to the plans God has for me. I know that he will never leave nor forsake me. I am also thankful to my mother and father as well as my entire family who has stuck with me throughout this journey.

My brother, Keion, and I have learned some great life-changing things that will stay with us for years to come. We heard specific stories of pain and success, life saving techniques in a health emergency, disciple and fitness, money awareness for our future and eye opening talks about our Manhood. I plan to share the experiences with my peers in school and all who I speak to. It's important for them to see good Godly character and as a leader; I know that my light must always shine.

I wish the graduating ROP Initiate Class of 2019 the best in their future paths. May the Word of God no longer be hidden in their hearts, but be the thing that saves them and keeps them from harm. I pray that we all seek God first in everything we do and never allow negative influences to impact our lives. I pray that we read the Bible daily and work to understand our purpose in life. I pray that we make our families and the ROP ministry proud that they poured into us.

With Gratefulness,
Corporal Keith Gregory Liburd, Jr.

ROP GRADUATION CEREMONY
Program Storyboard
[African Percussions begins playing]
WELCOME [Voice Over]
(Sheryl Lightsy)

"Welcome to the Rites of Passage Commencement Ceremony!" And now please receive our Village Pastor of Faithful Central Bible Church, Dr. John-Paul Foster... the Village Elders...the Village Instructors, Men of Valor, Village Champions, and the Alumni...the Village Parent Counsel...the Mothers and representing Parents...

PROCESSION
[In order, Pastor John-Paul Foster, Irving Tolbert and Village Elders, followed by Men of Valor and Champions, Parent Counsel, and the Mothers and representing Parents.]

PASTOR JORDAN ALLEN INTRO [V.O.]
(Sheryl Lightsy)

"Please welcome, one of our esteemed Village Pastors, Pastor Jordan Allen."
[Pastor Allen goes to podium.]

GRADUATES INTRODUCTION
(Pastor Jordan Allen)

"You may be seated."
[He introduces the Graduates.]
"And now, we present to you, the Rites of Passage Graduating Class of 2022."
THE GRADUATES PROCESSION
[The Graduates actually execute a coordinated procession march.]
OPENING PRAYER
(Pastor Jordan Allen)

After prayer..."You may be seated."
OCCASION
(Pastor Jordan Allen)

"We're here to celebrate the Rites of Passage journey to which these parents committed for these young men! Rites of Passage is Initiation Rites, which are performed to mark (symbolically) the passage from the stage of childhood to godly, young adulthood.

During this Passage, they were introduced to the physical, social, vocational, educational, spiritual responsibilities of manhood. This program was established here at Faithful Central Bible Church with leadership by the Village Elders, the wisdom of these life lesson Instructors and the support of the Men of Valor and Champions, with the cooperation of the Parent Counsel, and most importantly, with the commitment of their loving parents. At this time, Rites of Passage Chairman, Irving Tolbert, and the Village Elders will lead the next portion of this Commencement Ceremony."

HISTORY – Chairman, Village Elder IRVING TOLBERT
INSTRUCTORS/MEN OF VALOR RECOGNITION
(Village Elder Ron Williams)
"I would like the Instructors and Men of Valor to stand. Thank you for
your instruction and long-serving commitment. You may be seated."
CHAMPIONS RECOGNITION
(Village Elder Stephan Tucker)
"I would like the Champions to stand. This is a first year for many of you Champions. It's
been challenging, but you've stayed committed, and we thank you. You may be seated"
ALUMNI/FAMILY RECOGNITION
(Village Elder Victor Bullock)
"I would like the Alumni to stand. Likewise, it's been a challenging year,
but you've stayed committed, and we thank you. You may be seated. Family
members who sacrificed to wake up for the last eight months at 5:30am
and drive to the church attend sessions, we see you. Thank you."
PARENT COUNCIL INTRODUCTION
(Village Elder Carlos Ray)
"I would like the Parental Council to stand."
(Recognition of the Parent Council)

GRADUATE'S HEART AND HOPE STATEMENT
(Village Elders Lloyd Walker and Jay Tryon)
"I want to commend the Graduates for your effort."
"And we pray, hope, and trust that you will have success by practicing
all that you've learned during the ROP program."

A PARENT'S LOVE
(Village Elder Sgt. James Alexander)
"I would like the Father and Mother champions who made the commitment
to get these graduates up early on Saturdays, for eight months, to stand!"

COMEDIAN KENTE SCOTT INTRO [V.O.]
(Sheryl Lightsy)
"And now. With a unique Rites of Passage perspective…
Please welcome, Mr. Kente Scott!"
[Kente Scott steps to the stage.]
A Unique ROP Perspective
(Comedian Mr. Kente Scott)

THE MOTHERS CEREMONY
(Village Elder Jack Lightsy)
[He talks the Mothers and Initiates through ceremony.]

"The 'Rites of Passage' tradition originated on the continent of Africa. When a boy reached an age of awareness and independence, the boy's father and Elders would leave the village, with the boys. They would remain in the wilderness in order to train up these boys with the knowledge and life lessons to become a godly young man."

"The Mother's Ceremony symbolizes the nurturing mother's interaction when her son returns to the village. Let the Mother's Ceremony begin."

"Sons, you may address your mothers."

[Sons stand. Turn to their mothers or representing female parent). Sons extend hands to help mothers stand. Mothers stand, walk pass, then turn to face their sons. Sons turn, to face their mothers. VE talks.]

Village Elder Jack Lightsy

"Mothers, using your son's name, declare these words to your son…

"(Son's first name), you have now come forth as a young man. Seed of my womb (or your mother's womb), I now sow God's word into your spirit…"

ALL MOTHERS

"(Son's first name), you have now come forth as a young man. Seed of my womb/or your mother's womb, I now sow God's word into your spirit…"

Village Elder Jack Lightsy

"Mothers. Share a scripture you'd like to speak into your son's spirit."

[Mothers will recite chosen scripture.]

Village Elder Jack Lightsy

"Speak these words to your son…

[Mothers will say to their sons…]

"I pray that God's Word will direct your steps."

ALL MOTHERS

"I pray that God's Word will direct your steps."

[Mother presents a new Bible to her son. They hug their sons.]

Village Elder Jack Lightsy

"Sons. You may seat your mothers."

[Sons assist mothers to be seated. Sons then return to their seats.]

Song Selection
(Ms. Tia P)

INITIATION CEREMONY

(Pastor JP Foster)

[Pastor JP will ask the Initiates to stand. He will discuss the meaning of the elements—fire, incenses, chalk, wet seaweed, lemon, honey, salt, and oil.]

Part of the African Rites of Passage ritual is the Initiation Ceremony.

There are symbols that apply to the lives of you young men.

First of all, there's the symbol of *fire*—Fire brings light. Light our hope will guide you along your path every day of your life.

There's the symbol of *incense*—Incense symbolizes the wind. The Spirit of the Lord, the Bible says, is as a wind that blows as it chooses. The wind of the sovereign God will take you young men to the north, south, east, and west.

There's the symbol of *chalk*—That symbolizes the earth. One day we all will return to the earth. But it is the life that you young men live between now and eternity that matters for the kingdom of God.

There's the symbol of *wet seaweed*—The seaweed symbolizes water. For substance. Water symbolizes your thirst for righteousness. For it is only God who can quench your thirst for righteousness.

There's the taste of life in the form of bitter *lemon*—For the truth is that it does not matter where one begins in life. Somewhere along your path, life does bring forth bitterness.

And then, very quickly, followed by *honey*—For God is God enough, to even sweeten the bitterness in our lives.

There's the symbol of *salt*—Salt is a purifying agent. It also symbolizes the call of God on your lives, for Jesus says "You are the salt of the earth." You're called to be a purifying agent of righteousness wherever you go.

And finally, there's the symbol of *oil*—The anointing of the presence of the living God, the fresh anointing of God upon your lives. For God has sovereignly ordered your steps.

May God fill you with His presence and power to fulfill everything that He has ordained for you! With these symbols of life, you make the passage from boys to young men. As Paul says in I Corinthians 13:11, "When I was a child, I talked like a child, I thought like a child, I reasoned like a child. When I became a man, I put the ways of childhood behind me."

We celebrate this Rite of Passage. We salute these young men who were once boys. Please give them a hand!

[Afterwards, Pastor JP asks the Initiates to sit.]

PRESENTATION OF CERTIFICATES

(Village Elders Sgts. James Alexander, Dwayne Fuqua and Tomas Johnson, Village Elders Jimmy White, Sgts. Michael Strickland and Tim Scarlett) [Sgts announce Graduate names. VEs hand out and congratulate Graduates.]

ACKNOWLEGDMENTS/PLEDGES
(Village Elder Irving Tolbert)

PARENT/GUARDIAN, INITIATE, CHAMPION, AND VILLAGE PLEDGES
PLEDGES
[Pledges may be printed in the Program]

We have heard and witnessed the completion of a journey and transference from boyhood to manhood. Now let's focus on the future as we welcome the next group of boys who will begin their training.

PARENT PLEDGE
"Parents or Guardians please stand and answer Yes."

1. Do you pledge to give the Village Elders charge of your child so that we can instill in your son the tenets of manhood?
   Parents Answer YES
2. Will you support your child so that he can fulfill all program requirements?
   Parents Answer YES
3. Do you pledge your support, your time, and will you pray?
   Parents Answer: YES

NEW INITIATES PLEDGE
"Initiates please stand and answer, Yes."

Initiates will you submit to the teaching, instruction and correction of the village leadership?
   Boys Answer: YES

CHAMPIONS PLEDGE
"Champions please stand and answer, Yes."

1. Do you pledge to walk this journey with the initiates to champion them in spiritual growth and life development?
   Champions Answer: YES
2. Do you pledge your time, your energy, and will you pray?
   Champions Answer: YES

THE VILLAGE PLEDGE
"Congregation, please stand."

1. Will you walk uprightly before these young boys?
   Congregation answers: YES

2. Will you pray and ask God to use you to be a positive influence on the development of these boys as they journey into young adulthood?
   Congregation answers: YES

Special acknowledgements
BLESSING BY THE MINISTRY PASTOR OVERSEER/BENEDICTION
(Pastor John-Paul Foster)
Rev. Dr. John-Paul Foster speaks to the graduates, mothers and
their families, closing the ROP program in prayer.
[Photograph the Pastor with the graduates, Elders, MOV,
Champions, Instructors and Parent Council.]

The Author

Photo by Hugh Williams

For over 25 years, Elder Irving Tolbert, D.Div., has volunteered as Chairman of the Rites of Passage Ministry at Faithful Central Bible Church in Inglewood, CA, where Rev. Dr. John-Paul Foster is Pastor. In 2022, Dr. Tolbert was awarded an honorary doctorate from Bible Believers College in Los Angeles for serving the Lord 32 years as an elder and 24 years as Chairman of ROP.

Irving was drafted into the United States Navy during the Vietnam era, hence his love for the military. After his honorable discharge, he relocated from Kansas City to Los Angeles, where he attended California State University. In 2017, he retired from a banking industry career as a City National Bank Vice President. In addition to ROP, Irving's retirement years are sprinkled with golf and family trips at every opportunity.

Irving is married to La Verne Tolbert, Ph.D., who has written/edited several books. Dr. Tolbert's tenure as a Christian Education Pastor and Assistant Professor at Biola's Talbot School of Theology inspired her signature text, *Teaching Like Jesus*, after which she named her ministry. The couple resides in California and has two daughters, four grandsons, two granddaughters, and two great-grandchildren. Another great-grandchild is on the way.

Printed in the United States
by Baker & Taylor Publisher Services